When the Rain Speaks

Celebrating God's Presence in Nature

MELANNIE SVOBODA, SND

When the
RAIN
SPEAKS

Celebrating God's
Presence in Nature

TWENTY
THIRD *23rd*
PUBLICATIONS

I dedicate this book to my nieces and nephews:
Melannie Hartman, John Hartman, Lori Hartman Telesz,
Matt Hartman, Chris Hartman, Tony Svoboda,
John Svoboda, and Melissa Svoboda Wicker.
May they continue to cherish creation and
to pass on their love for nature
to the next generation.

Twenty-Third Publications
A Division of Bayard
One Montauk Avenue, Suite 200
New London, CT 06320
(860) 437-3012 or (800) 321-0411
www.23rdpublications.com

ISBN 978-1-58595-684-5
Library of Congress Catalog Card Number: 2007939318
Printed in the U.S.A.

Contents

Acknowledgments

I want to thank the following for their help in writing this book:

- My parents for instilling in me a love for nature at a very early age.

- My brothers John and Paul Svoboda and my sister Mary Ann Hartman for all the ways we shared our love for nature together over the years. I also want to thank them for verifying certain facts from my childhood for me.

- My nephew John Svoboda for clarifying information about gardening, bees, and mushrooms.

- The following Sisters of Notre Dame for advising me on certain aspects of this book: Sisters Alice Dugar, Margaret Hess, Sally Huston, and Lenette Marcello.

- My many good friends for accompanying me as I walked through parks, admired trees and flowers, sat by a lake, watched birds, visited the zoo, listened to spring peepers, and gazed at the moon and the stars.

- The environmental committee of the Sisters of Notre Dame for instilling in our province a greater appreciation of the natural world and for educating us on specific environmental issues.

- The various books, magazines, TV shows, and Web sites devoted to nature that I have enjoyed over the years, such as *Wild Kingdom, National Geographic Magazine, Animal Planet,* the *Discovery Channel,* and many more.

Introduction

I was born and raised on a small goose farm in Willoughby Hills, Ohio. It was here in northeastern Ohio, approximately five miles south of Lake Erie (as the goose flies), between the watersheds of the Cuyahoga and Chagrin Rivers, that I first became acquainted with the wonderful world of nature. Though our farm was small—a little over twenty-two acres—it had everything a child could want: an expansive lawn, a huge garden, an old orchard, several fields, and a dark, dense woods in the back. Within its borders were a large pond, a tiny creek that dried up every summer, two wells, and a bigger creek that meandered through our back woods.

Our family of six lived in a two-story yellow farm house with eleven rooms and three porches. When my parents purchased the farm for $6,000 in 1942, the house was already about sixty years old. Their money secured other buildings as well: a barn, a brown wooden chicken coop, a grey cinder block coop, a wooden garage that leaned east, and (my favorite!) a granary. I say "my favorite" because eventually my sister and I claimed half of the granary for a playhouse.

This was the setting in which I first experienced the world of nature: sunrise and sunset, the brightness of the day and the darkness of the night, the oppressive heat of summer and the biting cold of winter. It was here where I first became acquainted with an array of trees, flowers, bushes, and other plants, as well as animals. We had a number of animals. First, there were the geese—not merely a few of them but rather hundreds of them that we raised and sold in the ethnic neighborhoods of downtown Cleveland. Then there were the dozens of chickens that graciously provided us with fresh eggs every day. Numerous cats also sauntered in and out of my childhood—including Babs, Tommy, Meow, and Roger (named after Roger Maris). And of course there were the loyal dogs, which were our faithful companions on our various excursions into the wild: Duke (my Dad's hunting dog), Butchie (an English bulldog that came with the farm), Butchie II (a beagle), and Butchie III (a sickly boxer someone dumped off one day; my dad took him in and nursed him back to health).

In 1962 I left the farm, and at age seventeen, I went into the convent. In entering the Sisters of Notre Dame in Chardon, Ohio, I went from one farm to another. Our provincial center where I spent my first years as a sister, sat on 600 acres of land consisting of lawns, lakes, gardens, fields, meadows, and woods. This setting played a vital role in my early formation in religious life. Throughout my years as a sister, I have lived in many different places—cities, suburbs, rural areas—in several different states—Ohio, Pennsylvania, North

Carolina, Virginia, and Michigan. My speaking engagements have taken me to many other states as well. My time in community leadership blessed me with visits to countries such as Italy, Germany, India, Korea, and Uganda. But, no matter where I happened to be, the steady underlying pulsation of my life has always been my love for nature.

This love has prompted me to write *When the Rain Speaks: Celebrating God's Presence in Nature,* a series of reflections on various aspects of God's creation. We who are Christian have a long tradition of turning to nature in our quest for God. Writing over 1600 years ago, St. Augustine said, "If you have an eye for it, the world itself is a sacrament." At the same time, we are careful not to equate nature with God, always holding that God exists over and beyond anything we can experience in the natural world.

Many of the reflections in this book are the direct result of my personal engagements with nature: rain, trees, spiders, horses, kittens, and deer. Others grew out of articles and books I have read or movies and TV programs on nature that fascinated me: bees, giraffes, atoms, the human heart, the Grand Canyon, and a voyage into the cosmos. Still others are a blend of both personal experience and enthusiastic research: the sun, soil, snowflakes, and the pith of a feather.

When the Rain Speaks is intended to encourage and support your own experience with and meditation on nature. To facilitate this, each reflection begins with an appropriate quotation on the theme of the reflection. Each concludes with a question or two inviting your personal dialogue with the text. There is also a fitting scripture passage to ponder, as well as a brief prayer to carry with you throughout the day. The book lends itself to both private reflection and group sharing. An index at the end will help guide you to specific topics in the text.

I write this book out of a sense of profound gratitude for the gift of creation. But I also write it out of a sense of urgency. Father Thomas Berry, who has written extensively about nature, has said this: "Today, in the opening years of the twenty-first century, we find ourselves in a critical moment when the religious traditions need to awaken again to the natural world as the primary manifestation of the divine to human intelligence." He goes on to say that a lack of awareness of this divine manifestation in nature is a fatal flaw that can lead to ecological and environmental disasters. Father Berry continues: "We will not save what we do not love. It is also true that we will neither love nor save what we do not experience as sacred."

May this book help to reawaken our appreciation of the natural world as the manifestation of the Divine. And may this reawakening encourage us to seek ways to preserve this sacred gift for future generations.

1 The Ash Tree

Sometimes a tree tells you more than
you can read in books.

❧ CARL JUNG TO A COLLEAGUE

One of my fondest memories of our farm was a large white ash that grew on the east side of the house by the dining room porch. It was taller than our two-story house—probably about forty feet tall—with a "wing span" of about forty feet as well. The tree shielded the house from those cold east winds that kicked up periodically. During the hot summer months, its lush foliage provided cool shade for us and our house. But for me and my siblings, the ash tree was more than a buffer against wind and a provider of shade. It was a member of our family.

The tree was our playground. We often climbed up into its sturdy branches where we pretended the afternoon away.

Sometimes we imagined the tree was a huge cargo plane with only one of its four engines still sputtering. We marveled as my brothers skillfully brought the plane in for a landing every time. Or the tree was a tree house in which we lounged, giggled, and shared secrets. The tree measured our growth. One by one we all got tall enough to swing up onto its lower branches without a boost. It was a tower from which the brave among us would jump in our earnest yet futile attempts to fly. The tree was our personal set of monkey bars, providing us with numerous limbs to crawl up and dangle from. It was our lookout post from which we could see clear over to the next farm. And the ash tree was our hiding place when Mom was cooking up more chores for us to do.

And all the while, the tree just stood there. Solid. Rooted. Immovable. It never went anywhere. It never sought shelter from the storms. It was voiceless, too, speaking not one word to us. Day after day after day it welcomed us into its branches or under its shade with no questions asked. The tree was forgiving too. Often we took its presence for granted. More than once we nailed signs into its limbs, but it never retaliated. It was the silent sentinel of our childhood.

The tree was still standing when the nearby airport expanded and took our farm, burned our house down, and cleared the land for a golf course. Our old ash tree was felled, a victim to progress as so many other trees have been throughout history.

Sister Macrina Wiederkehr, a writer of many spiritual books, said that at one time in her life her spiritual director was a tree. That makes perfect sense to me, for I have always felt our ash tree, like many other trees, exuded a wisdom unsurpassed by most other living things.

To this day, I am amazed how a single tree could have had such an impact on my growing up. When I recall our ash tree, these images come effortlessly to mind: friend, playmate, confidant, shelter, sage, nanny, grandfather, even God. I regret that I never thanked the ash tree for all it did for me. Maybe this reflection is one small way I am doing that.

For Reflection/Discussion

- ❧ Are there any special trees in your life?
- ❧ Who has provided you with shelter and shade in your life?
- ❧ Have you ever been a tree for others?

Jesus said, "With what can we compare the kingdom of God, or what parable will we use for it? It is like a mustard seed, which, when sown upon the ground, is the smallest of all the seeds on earth; yet when it is sown it grows up and becomes the greatest of all shrubs, and puts forth large branches, so that the birds of the air can make nests in its shade." ❧ MARK 4:30–32

Maker of Trees, I thank you for all the silent, steady, growing things in my life.

2 Horses and Camels

*Look at practically anything...and see
that not only did the creator create
everything, but that he is apt to create
anything. He'll stop at nothing.*
❧ ANNIE DILLARD

For five years I lived in Middleburg, Virginia, in the heart of horse country. Though our school and convent had no horses, we were literally surrounded by them. Everywhere you looked, walked, or drove, you saw horses grazing in expansive fields or being ridden down back roads. In fact, across the road from us was a farm devoted to the training of racing horses. The place had twelve barns that housed about twenty horses each. For a horse lover like me, Middleburg was paradise.

I have always thought that the horse was one of the pinnacles of God's creation. Everything about a horse is beautiful: the line of its back, the shake of its mane, the flare of its nostrils, the glint in its large deep eyes, the curve of its flanks, the sheen of its coat. No matter what a horse is doing, it's beautiful, whether it's bending over to nibble some grass, trotting over to get a drink of water, running full speed down a race track, or just standing there.

How much more lovely the horse is than so many other four-legged creatures. Take the camel. Don't get me wrong now. I like camels. I think they're cute. But I sometimes imagine that the camel was God's first attempt at making a horse. After all, the camel does resemble the horse—except perhaps for its humps. Though the camel didn't turn out as pretty as God had envisioned, God decided to keep the camel anyway. God found its ungainliness endearing and useful. I can almost hear God saying to the first camel, "You're not exactly what I had in mind, but I'm going to keep you anyway. I've designed you for a unique task: desert travel. And, when my Son is born in Bethlehem, you will have a special role to play by carrying three Kings to pay him homage." Horses and camels. In God's creation, there's plenty of room for both.

For Reflection/Discussion

- How accepting are you of the "horses and camels" in your life?
- Do you ever find yourself judging by "appearances" alone? Have you ever been wrong?

"For everything created by God is good, and nothing is to be rejected, provided it is received with thanksgiving...."   ✽ 1 Timothy 4:4

Ingenious Creator, help me to appreciate both the horses and the camels in my life.

3 Cosmic Voyage

Remember the sky you were born under,
Know each of the star's stories.

> 🍂 JOY HARJO

NASA put out a movie recently called *Cosmic Voyage* narrated by Morgan Freeman. The first few minutes of the film take the viewer on a voyage to the outermost limits of the known universe. The distances portrayed are mind-boggling. We are reminded that the farthest we humans have ventured into space is 250,000 miles, the distance to the moon. Our sun, said to be a medium-sized star by star standards, is ninety-three million miles away and is so huge its diameter is two hundred and ten times that of earth's. The next nearest star to planet earth, Proxima Centauri, is about 4.2 light years away. Light, remember, travels at 186,000 miles per second! Traveling at the speed of our current rockets, it would take us 100,000 years to reach that nearest star.

Other facts are beyond comprehension. In our galaxy there are between fifty and one hundred million stars. And there are at least fifty billion other galaxies. And each one of these galaxies contains between ten million and 1 trillion stars! How old is the universe? The proponents of the Big Bang theory estimate it is 13.7 billion years old. How large is the universe? Most astronomers say it is trillions of light years across. What lies beyond the known universe? Nobody knows.

I sometimes show this movie when I facilitate retreats. After viewing this first part of the film, I invite the re-treatants to just sit in silence for a few minutes. Then I ask, "What are you thinking after viewing this? How are you feeling?" Usually my question is initially met with silence, not because people are afraid to speak, but because the film simply renders one speechless. After a few moments, some will begin to respond. Several simply shake their heads and say, "Wow!" One person said, "It certainly is humbling." Another said with wonder in her voice, "And yet the hairs on my head are numbered?" Still another expressed her baf-flement in this way: "This gives a whole new appreciation of the Incarnation. Given the expanse of the universe, how did Jesus ever find our galaxy, our solar system, our planet, Nazareth, Mary's womb?" But most often the response is simply, "What must God be like?"

For Reflection/Discussion

- ❧ Have you had an experience of the vastness of the universe? How did you react?
- ❧ How would you begin to answer the question: What must God be like?

(God) brought (Abram) outside and said, "Look towards heaven and count the stars, if you are able to count them." Then he said to him, "So shall your descendants be." And he believed the Lord; and the Lord reckoned it to him as righteousness.

❧ GENESIS 15:5–6

Creator of the Cosmos, may I ponder the stars regularly in my relentless quest to know who you are.

4 The Art of Beholding

Every creature in the world will raise our hearts to God if we look upon it with a good eye.

❧ ST. FELIX OF CANTALICE

One of my favorite words in the English language is *behold*. I admit it is something of an old-fashioned word. You don't hear too many people today saying, "Behold the sunset!" or "Behold the taxi!" We do find the word, however, in older translations of scripture where Jesus says things like, "Behold the lilies of the field!" And we come across it in old Christmas carols like "Behold that star!" The word essentially means "Look!" or "See!" But it connotes more than that. It implies wonder, regard, and awe. It says with excitement, "Look!" and then implies, "But do not touch!" or, if you do touch, "Do no harm!"

Some of us learn to behold quite young. A friend told me of her eight-year-old son Ryan who was playing with a couple of his friends on the playground one day, when they spotted a big spider scurrying across the asphalt. One boy said, "Let's kill it!" Ryan objected and said they should leave the spider alone because spiders are good for the environment. The other boys laughed at him and made fun of him. That evening, when Ryan tearfully told his mother what had happened on the playground, she said he had done the right thing to defend the spider and she was very proud of him. Though only eight, Ryan has already learned to behold.

Although the word is out-of-date, the concept should never be. There are many things in the world that we should simply "Behold!" Not everything we are afraid of needs to be killed. Not everything we think is ugly needs to be harmed or laughed at. Not everything needs to be analyzed, handled, or tinkered with either. Beholding is an attitude that needs to be taught and cultivated. How?

I remember when my niece Melissa met her first cat, Friskers, many years ago. She was only a toddler at the time, but when she spotted the cat by the living room couch, she immediately charged across the room, and before anyone could stop her, she had grabbed one of Frisker's ears. Her mother, running after her, cried, "No, Melissa! Don't hurt the kitty!" and swooped the cowering cat into her arms. Then her mother did something beautiful. She held the cat in front of Melissa and said, "Pet the kitty nicely, Melissa, like this." And she gently stroked the cat a few times, saying "Nice kitty! Nice kitty!" Melissa caught on right away. She too patted Friskers gently on top of his furry little head and said, "Nice kitty! Nice kitty!" Melissa was learning the art of beholding.

I have witnessed other parents teaching their children to behold. I have overheard them saying things like this to their little ones: "Nice doggie…, Pretty flower…, Good baby." Sometimes their lesson includes the extra admonition, "Now don't touch. Just look!"

Beholding lies at the heart of the spiritual life. In fact, it is the first step toward contemplation. What is contemplation but the prayerful attentiveness to something—a word in scripture, the blueness of an iris, a movement of one's spirit, the song of a chick-a-dee, the sound of rain tapping on a porch roof. My niece Lori shared an experience she had while changing the diaper of her newborn son. As she gazed at his umbilical cord one day, she was overcome with emotion when she realized that little Zachary had been attached to her for nine whole months! Through that cord, she thought, he had received all his nourishment from her. She told me her eyes welled with tears at the wonder of it. I knew Lori had experienced a profound contemplative moment, a moment made possible by her simple attentiveness to and beholding of her baby.

The English mystic Evelyn Underhill wrote: "For lack of attention, a thousand forms of loveliness elude us every day." Setting time aside each day to behold the many forms of loveliness all around us is one of the most important decisions we can make.

For Reflection/Discussion

- 🐦 What have you beheld today?
- 🐦 How did you share your wonder and awe?

Behold the works of the Lord....   🐦 PSALM 46:8

God of all loveliness, teach me to behold.

5 The Two-Thousand-Year-Old Seed

Who plants a seed
Beneath the sod
And waits to see
Believes in God.

🍂 ANONYMOUS

ecently I read that Israeli scientists have succeeded in getting a two-thousand-year-old date palm seed to germinate and produce a healthy sapling. (They appropriately nicknamed the sapling Methuselah.) Imagine: That seed lay dormant somewhere for two thousand years! No sun. No moisture. No conditions conducive to germination. But when the scientists provided the necessary conditions, the seed not only sprouted, it produced a sapling. I also learned that date palms are either male or female, and although researchers do not yet know the gender of the sapling, they are hoping it is a female so it will produce fruit. (I guess they will have to change its name to Methuselina!)

The researchers have another reason to be excited about the little sapling. Throughout the centuries, date palm trees have been known for their medicinal properties. The researchers are wondering if this particular sapling might have healing properties no longer found in today's date palm varieties. This story makes me wonder: What cures still lay undiscovered in the berries, leaves, and roots all over this planet?

For me that two-thousand-year-old date palm seed is a symbol of hope. I read somewhere that hope is "revolutionary patience." I like that. It reminds me that it takes considerable patience to be a person of hope. And it takes a ready willingness to work. Eric Fromm said that those whose hope is weak "settle down for comfort or violence." But those whose hope is strong "see and cherish all signs of new life." In addition, they are "ready at every moment to help the birth of that which is ready to be born."

For Reflection/Discussion

- ❧ To what extent are you a person of hope?
- ❧ Is there anything inside of you that could germinate given the proper conditions?

Very truly, I tell you, unless a grain of wheat falls into the earth and dies, it remains just a single grain; but if it dies, it bears much fruit.   ❧ JOHN 12:24

Seed Keeper, help me to discover the hidden
potential in myself and others today.
Share with me how I might make conditions
more conducive for germination.

6 The I-Wanna-Be-Outdoors Gene

I only went out for a walk, and finally concluded to stay out till sundown, for going out, I found out, was really going in.

🐾 JOHN MUIR

Cody, my two-year-old grandnephew, likes the outdoors. If he is inside the house and you ask, "Cody, wanna go outside?" his body begins to quiver with excitement and he immediately scampers to the door. Some days the weather is too nasty for him to go outside, so his parents had to put a little stool by the kitchen window for him. On those days, he stands on his stool and gazes longingly and lovingly at the outside world.

There is only one problem with taking Cody outside. Once he is there, he does not want to come back inside. When you tell him it is time to go in, he will fuss, dart away from you, and squirm and cry as you drag him back into the house. No one taught Cody to love the outdoors. It is part of his genetic makeup. Somewhere on some chromosome on some obscure gene is the *I-wanna-be-outdoors* hereditary trait. Our family is convinced this trait was passed down to Cody from his father (my nephew) who got it from his father (my brother) who got it from his father (my dad).

In ancient times, humans spent more time outdoors than indoors. Caves were places in which they merely slept or hid from prowling beasts. But as civilization progressed, humans began to spend more and more of their waking hours indoors. Today some people can go weeks without going outside except to scoot to work, church, or the grocery store. I have read that today the average American spends only ten minutes a day outside.

Consequently, we sometimes have to make the conscious effort to go outside for a while or at least to gaze out our windows. Why? Even little Cody already seems to know the answer to that question: There are lessons worth learning that only the outside can teach us. And by going outside, we find ourselves really going inside.

For Reflection/Discussion

🍃 Have you spent any time outside recently?

🍃 What lessons have you learned by being outside?

God saw everything that he had made, and indeed, it was very good.   🍃 GENESIS 1:31

God of Indoors and Outdoors, may I find traces of your presence wherever I go today.

7 Microcosmos

All you tiny things, bless the Lord.
🎬 ANONYMOUS AFRICAN CHANT

S everal years ago the French made a documentary film called *Microcosmos*, which is all about the life-and-death struggles going on in grassy meadows, algae covered ponds, forest floors, and desert sands. The movie features such creatures as snails, ants, butterflies, spiders, and (one of my personal favorites) dung beetles. One reviewer of the film, Anne Raver, describes the mating of two snails, saying the scene may very well be one of the most erotic love scenes in the history of film making. The two snails, which just happen to bump into each other in the grass one day, instantly begin to "make love." Raver writes: "After touching each other's faces with their little eye stalks for a split second, they glom on to each other, writhing and kissing for what seems like an eternity."

24

The film puts us nose to nose with the insect world. We see a lady beetle scurrying along a dew-laden blade of grass. We see ants washing each other's faces and sipping water from a puddle. We see a wasp emerging from an egg case and testing its wings. And we see a dung beetle pushing a ball of dung four times its size. When the ball gets stuck on a tiny stem jutting from the ground, the beetle pushes hard with everything it has. The ball doesn't budge. So the beetle turns over and tries pushing with its back legs. Still it doesn't budge. Finally the beetle goes around the ball, pushing from all sides, until the ball springs loose from the stem. The beetle continues to push the dung ball until (we suppose) it encounters the next obstacle.

The film is noteworthy for several reasons. First, it puts the viewer eye-to-eye with insects, a view we seldom have the opportunity to take. Secondly, it records the real sounds of the insect world. We actually hear the ants sipping that water. And thirdly, the film helps us appreciate all the hidden labors these insects perform day after day, year after year, century after century, millennium after millennium.

For Reflection/Discussion

❧ How can you meet an insect today?

❧ How can you stoop down or climb up and take a different perspective on one aspect of your world today?

Praise the Lord from the earth...
Wild animals and all cattle,
creeping things and flying birds! ❧ PSALM 148:7, 10

God of the Microcosmos, give me a greater appreciation of all that is small in my world.

8 Giraffe Design 101

Animals are here in part to grant
glimpses of the grace of beauty.

           ✿ MATTHEW FOX

*T*he basic design of the giraffe is quite remarkable. For one thing, giraffes have high blood pressure, about double that of human beings. The reason is simple. An adult giraffe's head is about six feet above its heart. If giraffes had the same blood pressure found in most animals, their blood would rise only part way up the neck and never reach the brain. But their unusually high blood pressure guarantees that the blood will get all the way up to the brain.

But with such high blood pressure, giraffes should have a terrible problem with swelling in their legs and feet. After all, the pressure that pushes the blood up to the brain is also pushing it down into the legs and feet. This great pressure, coupled with the pull of gravity, should cause immense swelling in their lower extremities. But giraffes don't walk around with swollen legs or feet. Why not? Because, as researchers discovered, giraffes have a "natural gravity suit." This means that their skin and other tissue in their legs are much stiffer and tougher than that of most animals. This toughness prevents their legs from swelling. In other words, the blood has no place else to go but back up to the heart.

But there is still another potential problem with the design of the giraffe. When giraffes bend over to drink, why doesn't the blood in their neck rush to their head? Here's another clever design gimmick that solves that problem. The giraffe's jugular vein, which carries blood from the head back to the heart, contains "flapper valves" that prevent the blood from flowing the wrong way. Human leg veins operate in much the same way. The jugular vein in the giraffe, like the leg vein in humans, has interior valves that allow blood to flow in only one direction—back to the heart. The giraffe is a marvel to behold—both on the outside and the inside!

For Reflection/Discussion

- ❧ What designs in nature intrigue you?
- ❧ Have you ever thought about, prayed about, the design of your own body?

O Lord, how manifold are your works!
In wisdom you have made them all;
the earth is full of your creatures.   ❧ PSALM 104:24

*Designer of All, give me the gift of ingenuity
to face the challenges in my life.*

9 When the Rain Speaks

We wait for the word of the Lord as we wait for the rains, and our God shall come down upon us like gentle dew.

❧ MONASTIC LITURGY

ain talks. If we listen carefully, we can hear what she has to say. Sometimes Rain sneaks up on us. We step outside to go to our mailbox, and halfway there we put out our hands—palms up—and say to ourselves, "It's raining!" We had not even noticed her gentle presence in the air, more like a mist than discernible drops. That is when we can hear Rain saying, "Gotcha!" as if pleased with her ability to completely envelope us without our even realizing it.

Most times Rain is more articulate. We hear her gentle pitter-patter on our roof in the morning while still in bed. That pitter-patter, enticing us to stay-in-bed, stay-in-bed, stay-in-bed, is more seductive than the song of any sea nymph. But the command of our conscience is usually louder. "GET UP!" it bellows, and so we do. Usually. Once up and dressed, we search for our umbrella. We pride ourselves if it is right where it should be, and blame the whole household if it is no-where to be found. Once in our car, we are forced to turn our windshield wipers from intermittent to low. All day long this gentle yet steady Rain speaks soothing words to our souls, saying, "Slow down…slow down…slow down."

Sometimes Rain is more dramatic. She comes gushing down so hard we wonder if we should start building an ark. Rain turns the driveway into a stream and the street into a mini river. The branches of the trees bow down low under the weight of all the water on their leaves. Puddles form everywhere, even in places we had assumed were straight and smooth—like parking lots. Rain reveals the illusion of level-ness. She pounds down the peonies so low we are sure they will never rise again. But somehow they do. Another illusion dispelled: Some things—like peonies—are not as fragile as they look.

Sometimes Rain shouts. She comes accompanied by her back-up rock band: Wind, Thunder, and Lightning. And boy, can they put on a show—especially their drummer, Thunder. When the band is performing with Rain, it is best to seek shelter inside. And stay there. Better yet, hunker down for a while until Rain and her band have played themselves out. There is no use arguing or fighting with Rain when she is in her shouting mood. What she is really saying amid all the noise is this: "Lay off!"

Rain is most welcome during a drought when the grass is brown, the leaves are shriveled, and the soil is cracked wide open. That is when we beg her to come, even falling down on our knees or performing ceremonial dances or promising God a hundred different things if only Rain would come. At these times, we anxiously eye the western sky, and if we see clouds forming in the distance, we ask one another in hushed tones, "Do you think there's rain in those clouds?" We ask cautiously, for the lack of Rain turns all of us into beggars. Though we humans have been dealing with Rain for thousands of years, none of us yet knows her mind. During severe drought, we all begin to believe she has abandoned us forever and is never coming back. But Rain usually does—though not always. It's sobering to think that some of today's deserts were yesterday's lush forests.

Sometimes Rain overextends her stay. She hangs on and on and on. Once again, we get down on our knees or do our dances or make promises to God if only Rain would go away. In the meantime, trickling creeks become gushing rivers, rivers overflow their banks, and people and animals are forced to evacuate homes, burrows, tunnels, dens, nests, and even trees. Rain makes fugitives of us all. She is relentless at times, wielding the power to disrupt the daily life of neighborhoods, towns, and even entire cities, reminding all of us how little control we have over anything. Rain humbles us. Once her mind is made up to stay, all we can do is pack up, flee to higher ground, come back when she's gone, and salvage what we can. During these times, Rain sometimes speaks one word to us: "Priorities."

Yes, Rain talks. When she speaks, she has much wisdom to share with us. In some ways, Rain reminds me of God.

For Reflection/Discussion

- ❧ What has Rain ever said to you?
- ❧ In what ways in your opinion is Rain like God?

May my teaching drop like the rain,
my speech condense like the dew;
like gentle rain on grass,
like showers on new growth. ❧ DEUTERONOMY 32:2

*Rain Maker, drench me with
your wisdom and love.*

10 What's the Matter?

I worship the Creator of matter, who became matter for my sake, who willed to take His abode in matter, who worked out my salvation through matter. Never will I cease honoring the matter which wrought my salvation.

❧ St. John of Damascus

*I*n 450 B.C., a Greek philosopher named Democritus theorized that all matter was composed of tiny particles eventually called atoms. The word atom comes from the Greek word *atomos* meaning indivisible or uncuttable. The existence of atoms wasn't scientifically confirmed until 1803 by a man named John Dalton. Over ninety years later, another scientist, J.J. Thomson, discovered that atoms were *not* indivisible. In fact they were composed of even tinier particles: electrons (discovered by Thomson), protons, and neutrons. In a way, a single atom looks like an itsy-bitsy, teeny-weeny solar system. The protons and neutrons form the core or nucleus of the atom (the sun) while the electrons (like planets) orbit the nucleus.

Today we know there are even smaller particles than electrons, protons, and neutrons. Some are called quarks. Scientists have identified six types of quarks and have given them these rather prosaic names: up quark, down quark, strange quark, charm quark, bottom quark, and (you guessed it) top quark. In addition to quarks, there are dozens of other subatomic particles including photons and neutrinos. There seems to be no limit to smallness.

All atoms are not created equal. They differ according to their structure. An atom that cannot be separated into different substances except by nuclear disintegration is called an element. Over the years, scientists have identified these various elements and arranged them on an orderly chart called the periodic table. Each element was given a symbol (Au is gold, Cu is copper, for example), an atomic number (helium is 2, platinum is 78) and an atomic weight (boron is 10.82, titanium is 47.90). There were 47 known elements in 1809. At this writing there are 117.

The elements possess an amazing property called bonding. This means they like to get together—not just for a cup of coffee. It's more like a marriage. When the elements get together they form compounds. When two hydrogen atoms, for example, bond with one oxygen atom they form the compound we call water (H_2O). When one sodium atom bonds with one chloride atom they form the compound salt (NaCl). Compounds are the basic building blocks of everything that exists: air, fire, rocks, stars, willow trees, ladybugs, eels, storks, otters, hippos, and human beings. Essentially, everything in creation is composed of the same "stuff," a fact that should make us humans more respectful of creation and more understanding of one another, don't you think?

Chemically speaking, human beings are composed of over forty-seven elements. Here are a few of those elements and their percentage of the human body: oxygen (65%), carbon (18%), calcium (1.5%), potassium (.2%), sodium (.15%), copper (.0001%), arsenic (.000026%), gold (.000014%), and radium (.00000000000000001%). The complete list of elements shows that, chemically speaking, we humans are not worth very much—only a buck or two, depending on inflation.

It is interesting to note that when elements get together and form a compound, the compound is more than the mere addition of the bonding elements. Take sugar. Sugar is composed of twelve parts carbon, twenty-two parts hydrogen, and eleven parts oxygen. Yet none of these elements by itself has the property of sweetness! But put them together and you get sweetness. In other words, when you combine some elements, you get more than the sum of the parts. (I have experienced this same phenomenon while working together with other people on a committee. Sometimes the result *is* greater than the sum of the committee's parts!)

Even a cursory look at atoms and elements can elicit wonder in us: The wonder of the atom itself, the wonder of bonding, the wonder of each element, the wonder of the connectedness of everything that exists. As with smallness, there seems to be no limit to wonder.

For Reflection/Discussion

🍂 What strikes you most in this reflection on matter?

🍂 Have you ever considered yourself as made up of elements?

Your way, O God, is holy.
What god is so great as our God?
You are the God who works wonders;
you have displayed your might among the peoples.

🍂 PSALM 77:13–14

Creator of All, I thank you that I am wonderfully made. And I thank you that everything else is wonderfully made too!

11 The Hawk Knows His Business

I confess that I have always longed for a glimpse of (God), but what I come up with time and again is a small revelation contained in some particular. A single forget-me-not, a hawk, a gnarled oak suddenly becomes luminous, weighty, saturated with meaning.

❧ SAM KEEN

While living in his hermitage in the Kentucky woods, the Trappist Thomas Merton had a lot of time to pray, write, and observe nature. In his journals, he describes some of his encounters with the wildlife that surrounded him.

One day he saw a pasture filled with migrating starlings. He watched them moving about and singing for about five minutes. He writes, "Then, like lightning, it happened....They opened their wings and began to rise off the ground and, in that split second, from behind the house and from over my roof a hawk came down like a bullet, and shot straight into the middle of the starlings just as they were getting off the ground." The hawk nails one of the birds with his talons. Merton continues, "It was a terrible and yet beautiful thing, that lightning flight, straight as an arrow."

Merton watched the hawk devour its prey saying, "He did not fly off with it like a thief. He stayed in the field like a king." Later Merton reflects further on the "sure aim" of the hawk, and suggests that the hawk should be studied by saints and contemplatives. He says admiringly, the hawk "knows his business. I wish I knew my business as well as he does his."

Part of the beauty and wonder of the natural world is the way things "know their business." They know who they are. They know what they are about. Snapdragons know what it means to be snapdragons. Goldfinches are good at being goldfinches. Leopards know what "leopardness" is all about. To Meister Eckhart, a thirteenth-century German mystic, this "knowing their business" was called *isness*. He maintained that *isness* is noble, and no creature is so insignificant that it lacks it.

For us humans, however, knowing our business, getting in touch with our *isness* is neither simple nor easy. Who are the humans who know what it really means to be human?

Babies do. Notice how all babies instinctively know how to suck and how to wail when something is not quite right.

All babies cry and coo in the same language. They crawl and toddle pretty much the same way no matter where they live—be it Perth, Oslo, Shanghai, or Nairobi. Babies know how to be babies, and children, children. It's we adult humans who often don't know our business, our *isness*.

And what is our business? Ultimately, it is to seek and find God. In his journal, Merton suggests that saints and contemplatives are closest to knowing the business of being human. Like the hawk, they fly with lightning speed, straight as an arrow, sure of their aim. And their aim is always God. If only we all could be as swift and as sure as that hawk.

For Reflection/Discussion

- What is your "business"? Are you able to articulate it?
- How swift and sure are you? What is your life goal?

God asks Job:
"Is it by your wisdom that the hawk soars,
and spreads its wings toward the south?
Is it at your command that the eagle mounts up
and makes its nest on high?"   Job 39:26–27

Author of Life, guide me in my seeking,
speed me in my flight to you.

12 Shedding

The fruit of letting go is birth.
✔ MEISTER ECKHART

S ome things in nature shed. Take trees. The sycamore tree sheds its bark every year, as does the birch. We humans sometimes use the shedding barks of trees to make things. Native Americans used the bark from birch trees to fashion their canoes. Today we still make bottle corks from the bark of the cork oak tree. We weave other bark fibers into cloth such as flax, hemp, and ramie. We also harvest things like gum and latex from the barks of other shedding trees. We even eat the perfumed bark of Sri Lankan saplings—better known as cinnamon.

Trees are not the only things that shed. Animals do too. In the animal world shedding is called molting. Molting is the routine shedding of feathers in birds, old hairs in mammals, old skin in reptiles, and the entire exoskeleton in arthropods.

First the birds. The molting in birds is a rather slow process compared to molting in other animals. Birds cannot shed their feathers all at once or they would not be able to fly. Besides, if they were featherless, they would freeze to death in chilly weather. So birds shed old feathers only a couple at a time. When an old feather falls out, a new pin feather grows where the old feather used to be. When the pin feather becomes a full feather, another old feather will fall off. Molting in birds seems quite orderly. But it does take time.

Many mammals shed their winter coats when spring comes around. Cat and dog owners know what a pain this can be as they run around the house sweeping up hairs from the floor and using a sticky-thingamajig to get the hairs off the couch before the company arrives.

Some reptiles, like snakes, shed their skin in order to grow. A typical snake sheds its skin by rubbing itself against something like a rock or a tree. Usually the skin comes off in one piece—starting with the head. It is a little like taking off a sock. Arthropods such as beetles, shed their entire exoskeleton, a fancy word for shell. Though beetles never get too big for their britches, they do get too big for their shells. Thus shedding enables them to grow.

What about us humans? Believe it or not, we too shed. In fact the top layer of our skin sheds about every two weeks. We are constantly getting new hairs too—unless, of course, we are bald.

Shedding is a good image for spiritual growth. When plants and animals are shedding, they are sloughing off their former selves. As we grow spiritually, we too might have to shed. Shed what? We shed things like ideas, attitudes, unhealthy behaviors, and even parts of our former selves.

For Reflection/Discussion

- Have you ever considered shedding a fear of growth? Why or why not?
- Is there anything you must shed at this particular time in your life to allow for the growth of a new and better you?

For his sake I have suffered the loss of all things, and I regard them as rubbish, in order that I may gain Christ....   PHILIPPIANS 3:8

Creator God, help me to shed whatever
hinders me from growing in
love and compassion.

13 Bees

*There is nothing but mystery in the
world, how it hides behind the fabric
of our poor, brownbeat days, shining
brightly, and we don't even know it.*

> 🐝 *THE SECRET LIFE OF BEES*
> BY SUE MONK KIDD

I was reading about bees the other day. I learned there
are over 20,000 species of bees. So if you have seen
one bee, you have *not* seen them all! You still have
19,999 more to go! The smallest bee, the dwarf bee, is 2.1 mm
or 5/64 of an inch. The largest bee, named Megachile Pluto,
is 39 mm or 1.5 inches. (The name is longer than the bee!)
Despite the various species and sizes of bees, almost all bees
share this trait: their antennae have thirteen segments if they
are male bees and twelve if they are females. No one is quite
sure why.

The oldest bee fossil is one hundred million years old. That fact alone increases my respect for bees. Look how long they have been on earth doing their bee thing. We humans did not appear on earth until (most scientists think) a mere three hundred thousand or so years ago! We and not bees are the new kids on the block (or should I say orb?). Although it is true that most bees can sting, they do so mainly to protect themselves. (Admit it! We use our stingers when we feel threatened too!) Bees are our friends. Their main gift to Planet Earth is pollination. One-third of the world's food supply depends on insects for pollination, a task done largely by bees. If anything were to happen to our bee population, our food supply would be seriously jeopardized.

Bees do not pollinate intentionally though. Rather, pollination is a by-product of their visits to flowers to collect nectar to take back to their hive. Collecting nectar is risky for bees, for it forces them to leave the security of their hive and their community. It exposes them to dangers of all sorts from predators to barefoot children. As one scientist put it, "Visiting flowers is a dangerous occupation with high mortality rates." But the bees are programmed to visit flowers and gather nectar in order to extend the life of the bee community into the future.

In addition to their gift of pollination, bees also give us honey. Honey is the sweet, thick liquid produced by bees from the nectar of flowers. It is the bees' food supply when the weather turns cold or when other food sources are scarce. Successful beekeepers encourage overproduction of honey in their bees, so the beekeeper can harvest some of the honey without endangering the bees.

Honey is a fascinating product. Once the bee returns to the hive with the nectar it has collected, it ingests it into its "honey stomach" and regurgitates it several times before depositing it into one of the honeycombs for storage. This means honey is really partially digested nectar. (I wonder how many honey lovers know this?) Honey is fascinating for another reason: it will not spoil. This is due to honey's high sugar content and low moisture content. Honey, therefore, has a very long shelf life. Not all honey is the same either. The specific composition of honey depends largely on the flower nectar consumed by the bees to make the honey. Anther important fact: honey can be harmful or even fatal to infants. We must never give honey to a child under eighteen months old.

Today we use honey mainly for food. We cook with it, spread it on our bread, and dissolve it in our tea. But in ancient times honey was frequently used for medicinal purposes. Open wounds were spread with honey to deter infection. Because honey is an excellent preservative, the ancient Egyptians and other peoples used honey for embalming purposes.

Bees are a symbol of the small things in nature that play a huge role in the well-ordering of life. For million of years bees have gone about their business of collecting nectar and making honey. In the process they have been pollinating many of the earth's plants that supply other animals—including humans—with life-sustaining food.

For Reflection/Discussion

- ❧ What other small things in nature play a big role in the well-ordering of life?
- ❧ What risks are you willing to take to nurture the communities to which you belong?

The precepts of the Lord are right,
rejoicing the heart...
sweeter also than honey,
and drippings of the honeycomb.   ❧ PSALM 19:8, 10

Loving God of Small Creatures, help me to notice small things today and to take nothing for granted.

14 Taming Things

It is the essence of faith to let God be God.

            ❧ JON SOBRINO, SJ

Since I lived on a farm as a child, my idea of a summer vacation was going to the city. So every summer I packed a little suitcase and went off to Cleveland (East 65th and Engel) to spend a week with my Aunt Mae and Uncle Ed. Since they had no children of their own, they doted on me. I was happy to accommodate their need to lavish some sweet child with affection.

One thing I liked about the city were the squirrels. On the farm, we did not have any squirrels living near the house. The presence of our dogs deterred them from nesting in any of the trees in our yard. Consequently, the only squirrels I ever saw at home were in the woods. And they tended to be elusive. But here in the city, the squirrels were all over the place—and practically tame. That was because my aunt fed the squirrels every day—often peanuts—right from her hand. As I watched the squirrels scamper up onto the back porch and cautiously snatch the peanut from Aunt Mae's outstretched hand, I thought, "Cool!" As an adult, I now have misgivings about feeding squirrels this way.

My recollection of those city squirrels got me to thinking how we humans have a proclivity for taming things. We like to get others—people, animals, plants, or rivers—to do what we want them to do, to behave in a way that pleases us. We achieve success in taming things—especially animals—by using some sort of incentive, usually food, a pat on the head, or affirming words. "Nice, doggie. Here's a biscuit for you... Nice, horsie, here's a carrot." Sometimes in our desire to be in control of animals, we forget that all wild animals are still wild no matter how "tame" they may appear to be. More than one lion tamer has been mauled by a lion he thought he had tamed. We can be misled in our approach to other wild animals too. A photographer recently got too close to a grazing buffalo in Yellowstone. The bull charged the man and he was killed. Similarly a man near Cleveland was recently killed by his "pet" boa.

Naturalists who work with wild animals work hard *not* to tame them—especially if they intend to release the animals back into the wild. These people know there is something unnatural and or even unhealthy about a tame bear, a domesticated cougar, or a well-behaved eagle. Recently I saw a program where animal researchers were trying to keep alive

an orphaned baby condor. To feed the fledgling, the researchers fashioned a glove puppet that looked just like an adult
condor—complete with eyes and beak. The baby condor received all of its food from its "puppet parent," never coming
in direct contact with any human.

This is not to say that all taming is wrong. Throughout
history humans have greatly benefited from the taming of
certain animals. How different the history of the world would
be if it were not for the taming of horses, for example. How
lonely many people would be without their pet dog or cat.
Yet, should seals be made to balance balls on their noses?
Should dogs be made to ride little bicycles? Should elephants
be made to stand on their hind legs?

And what about people? Do we humans ever try to tame
other humans? Sometimes we do. We can make the mistake
of thinking of our loved ones as our "possessions." Many a
marriage has failed because one spouse has entered into the
marriage with the goal of taming the other. Parents can exert
too much control over their children too. Yes, we must edu-
cate the next generation, even "domesticating" them, if you
will. But hopefully we will do so without taking away each
child's individuality, spunk, or spark.

And what about God? Do we ever try to tame even God?
Sometimes I am afraid we do. Every time we try to get God
to do what we want, to run the world as we see fit, or even
to leave us well enough alone, aren't we trying to tame God?
We may not toss God a bone or a carrot, but we might toss
God a special prayer, a particular penance, or a promise in

an attempt to bend God's will our way. But, hopefully, sooner or later we realize that there is something unnatural and unhealthy about a domesticated God too. Nature reminds us that some things will not be tamed—and rightfully so.

For Reflection/Discussion

- 🐦 Have you ever tried to tame someone or something?
- 🐦 Do you ever try to tame God? In what particular ways?

Can you draw out Leviathan with a fish-hook,
or press down its tongue with a cord?
Will it make a covenant with you
to be taken as your servant for ever?   🐦 Job 41:1, 4

O Tameless One, help me to relate
to you and others with freedom and love.

15 The Sun

*I saw the red flame of the kingly sun
glaring through the black trees, not like
dawn but like a forest fire. Then the sun
became distinguished as a person and
he shone silently and with solemn power
through the branches, and the whole
world was silent and calm.*

🌿 THOMAS MERTON

*H*uman beings have always been fascinated by the sun. Many ancient civilizations (such as the Incas of South America and the Aztecs of Mexico) actually worshipped the sun as a god. A number of ancient monuments were constructed specifically with the sun in mind. Stonehenge in England, for example, accurately marks the summer solstice. Many pyramids in Egypt were also built in direct reference to the sun.

The ancient Greeks thought the sun was one of seven planets that revolved around Earth. After all, it appeared to the naked eye that the sun did go around Earth. In many languages (including English) a day of the week is named in honor of the sun: Sunday. The ancient Romans revered the sun so much they imprinted its image on some of their coins. In the fourth century, Christians chose December 25 to celebrate the birthday of Jesus. This date had been a pagan holiday that honored "the undefeated sun." Because of their belief in Jesus' resurrection, Christians stole the date for Christmas and began to call Jesus "the undefeated sun."

It is easy to see why the ancients worshipped the sun. By all standards, it is a marvel. The sun, as we know, is a star—a medium-sized star, astronomers tell us. But that designation is misleading. By mass, the sun is in the top ten percent of the stars in our galaxy. But the fact remains, some stars, like the red supergiant star Betelgeuse in the constellation Orion, dwarf the sun in size. If Betelgeuse were put into the center of our solar system, its outer surface would extend between the orbit of Mars and the orbit of Jupiter!

The sun is the center of our solar system. It contains 99% of the mass of our entire solar system. (Jupiter contains most of the rest.) The sun is so huge, its interior could hold 1.3 million earths! The sun is hot too. (That's an understatement!) Its surface temperature is 5,500 Kelvins. On the Kelvin scale, water boils at a temperature of 373.13, as compared to Fahrenheit (211.97) and Celsius (99.98). The core of the sun is even hotter: 13,600,000 Kelvins! The sun is so hot, it is really white. But atmospheric conditions make it appear yellow to us earth viewers. (When writing about the sun, one is tempted to use exclamation points after every single sentence!)

The sun is a third-generation star. This means it came from another star (a parent star), which came from another star (the sun's grandparent). The sun has a life cycle, much as we do. Scientists estimate that the sun is 4.57 billion years old. They also say that it is about halfway through the "main-sequence evolution stage." In approximately four to five billion years, the sun will enter a new phase (it's something all stars go through) called the "red giant phase." Unfortunately for planet earth, when the sun enters this phase, there will be catastrophic consequences for our world. For one thing, the sun will boil away all of earth's water.

For now, however, the energy from the sun supports virtually all life on earth through the process of photosynthesis. (See the chapter on photosynthesis.) That same energy drives the earth's climate and weather. Though scientists have studied the sun quite extensively, they still have many unanswered questions—especially concerning sunspots, solar flares, and solar wind.

It takes a poet, however, to begin to capture in words the magnificence of the sun. Francis Thompson, who lived in Victorian England, was such a poet. It was the sun that occasioned a profound religious experience for Thompson as he was staying at a monastery recovering from an opium addiction. As he watched the setting sun, Thompson felt a rebirth within himself of both his poetic powers and his relationship with Christ. He saw in the setting sun a mystical symbol of Christ's death and resurrection. In his poetry, he speaks of the sun's "radiant finger," "burning curls," "sceptered beam," and "unattainable wing." In "Ode to the Setting Sun," he says to the sun, "Thou dost image, thou dost follow / That King-Maker of Creation… / Thou art of Him a type memorial."

For Reflection/Discussion

- Have you thanked God for the sun lately?
- How is the sun a good image of God for you?
- How is the sun a good image of Jesus?

From the rising of the sun to its setting
the name of the Lord is to be praised. PSALM 113:3

*Creator of Our Sun, help me to see and feel the
light and warmth of your love.*

16 John Muir

The ability to see beauty is the begin-
ning of our moral sensibility. What we
believe is beautiful we will not wantonly
destroy.

❧ Rev. Sean Parker Dennison

John Muir is one of the earliest modern conservation-
ists. Born in Scotland in 1838, he immigrated to the
United States with his family in 1849, settling on a
farm in Portage, Wisconsin. While attending the University
of Wisconsin, he signed up for a botany course. This course
proved to be a turning point in his life. In his biography, he
describes one of those botany classes held under a towering
locust tree. A fellow student plucked a flower from the tree
and explained how the locust tree was a member of the pea
family. Muir writes, "This fine lesson charmed me and sent
me flying to the woods and meadows in wild enthusiasm."

Muir dropped out of college and enrolled in "the university of the wilderness." He walked one thousand miles from Indiana to Florida, enjoying and studying nature the entire way. Because of a bout with malaria, Muir was prevented from walking all the way to South America as he had planned to do. Instead, he walked to California where he worked at various jobs to support himself. Muir saw nature not merely as a practical benefit for humankind—trees to give us lumber, mountains to give us coal. He saw nature as something valuable for its own sake. He also appreciated nature for the spiritual qualities it possessed. Seeing Yosemite for the first time, he wrote: "No temple made by hands can compare with this."

Muir was also keenly sensitive to the connectedness of all things, writing, "When we try to pick out anything by itself, we find it hitched to everything else in the universe." He fought to preserve areas from development. The preservation of Yosemite as a national park is one of his greatest achievements. He also founded the Sierra Club, which continues to be one of the most important conservation organizations in the United States.

Muir's letters, essays, and books are still widely read today. His love for nature resonates with the minds and hearts of many people. One of my favorite quotes of this remarkable man is this: "Everyone needs beauty as well as bread, places to play in and pray in, where nature may heal and give strength to body and soul alike."

For Reflection/Discussion

- What spiritual qualities do you find in nature?
- Has nature ever healed you or given strength to your body and soul?

Great is the Lord, and greatly to be praised;
his greatness is unsearchable.   ✤ PSALM 145:3

*God of the Wilderness, may your creation give
healing and strength to my body and soul.*

17 To the Kitten I Killed

There is only one thing harder in this world than forgiving. It's to ask forgiveness armed only with, "I'm sorry."

🐾 ERMA BOMBECK

ear Kitten,

I'm sorry. I never meant to kill you. It was an accident. A terrible accident. I was only eight at the time and I loved kittens. Honest. We always had kittens on our farm. And a few cats too. I loved kittens and cats back then. And I still do.

But it happened one lazy summer day. I was out playing by myself in one of the back fields when I spotted you. You were small, but not too small, and you were a pretty black and white. Right away I knew you were not one of my kittens. I knew all my kittens very well. Maybe I wanted to catch you and bring you home. Maybe I just wanted to pet you. I can't recall now. But, seeing you, I darted toward you and you ran away. So I ran after you. Across the grassy field the two of us ran, you in the lead but me in hot pursuit.

Then it happened. You stopped. Dead in your tracks. No warning. You just stopped. But I didn't stop. I couldn't. I was running too fast. Before I knew what had happened, my one foot came down hard—very hard—on your furry little body. I was horrified. By the time I stopped my momentum and looked back at you, you were lying there, writhing. I won't say any more than that. I knew I had hurt you. Badly.

Instantly I started to scream and cry, afraid to touch you or even go near you. My brother Paul heard the commotion all the way from the barn and came running out to see what was wrong. Through my sobs, I pointed to you and told him what happened. Although he was only a year older than me, he took charge with a maturity beyond his years. He kept saying, "It was an accident. It was an accident." Then he told me to go away and he'd take care of everything. Sobbing, I walked away—slowly at first and then I ran. I knew you would not live. You were going to die. I had killed you.

You did die. Paul buried you. And that was that.

Only it wasn't that simple. Although your death occurred many, many years ago, it touched me deeply. So deeply, I still wince whenever I think about it. Although I had seen other animals die before you, and I have seen other animals die since, your death stands out because of my complicity in it. I killed you. Yes, yes, it was an accident, but I still killed you.

I learned many things the day you died. I learned I can inflict serious harm on someone or something without intending to do so. When this happens, asking for forgiveness is the only recourse that brings any modicum of peace. I also learned how fragile life can be. One minute you were alive and running, the next you were dying and dead. And I also learned how precious all life is—even the life of one nameless, little kitten, you.

Once again, I'm sorry. Please forgive me.

Sincerely, Melannie

For Reflection/Discussion

- ❧ Do you owe an apology to anything in creation?
- ❧ Have you ever accidentally killed or harmed an animal, a tree, a bird, a person?

To the Lord our God belong mercy and forgiveness....

❧ DANIEL 9:9

Loving God, teach me to be gentle with all forms of life. And help me, if necessary, to say, "I'm sorry."

18 The Way Things Get from Here to There

Praise incessantly, hold high expectations, laugh, sing out loud, celebrate without ceasing the good luck of getting set down here on a lively earth.

ʂ Barbara Kingsolver

*G*od the Creator got a little carried away when it came to the ways animals move. In biology, the study of animal movement is called locomotion. Simply put, locomotion is the self-powered, patterned motion of limbs or other body parts by which an individual customarily moves from one place to another. All the words in that definition are important. Locomotion must be *self-powered*. If you are shot out of a cannon, that is not locomotion (although it is a little loco!). Locomotion must be the way the individual *customarily* moves. If you fall down the stairs head first, that is not locomotion either, because that is not your customary way of going down the stairs. At least I hope it isn't.

Biologists divide locomotion into categories such as walking, running, crawling, climbing, swimming, and aerial movement. Each of these categories is further divided into sub-categories. Aerial movement, for example, includes falling, parachuting, gliding, flying, and soaring. There are other factors of locomotion that are interesting—at least to biologists. The difference between walking and running is not merely speed. Running begins when both feet (in humans, at least) are off the ground simultaneously. (There are different standards for quadrupeds.) Biologists have strict ways of differentiating slithering from climbing from scrambling. For the records, snakes are slitherers, lemurs are climbers, and mountain goats are scamperers.

Which brings us to legs. Legs were a marvelous invention. But here again God got carried away giving creatures various numbers of legs. We humans, of course, fall into the category of bipeds, two-legged creatures. We share this category with all birds, several other mammals, and a couple of lizards. You might be wondering, is there a uniped (one-legged) category? Yes there is. And in that category is the springtail which is really a hexapod (six-legged), but doesn't belong to the insect family because it has an internal mouth rather than an external one. The springtail (as its name suggests) uses its tail as a leg—something like a pogo stick—to get from one place to another. BOING! The springtail needs locomotion, because, I'm sure, it has urgent business to attend to just as we do.

The next category (according to the number of legs) is the quadruped (four-legged), the largest category of animals. (You are probably thinking, "You skipped the tripods!" No, as far as I can tell there are no tripods in nature. (Tripods are all made by humans to support their cameras.) Some quadrupeds walk, but many of them hop. Next come the insects, the hexapods (six-legged). Not all insects walk on all six of their legs. The Praying Mantis, for example, walks on only four of its six legs, using the other two legs as arms. The octopods (eight-legged) come next. These, of course, include spiders and the octopus. Other creatures have even more than eight legs. The woodlouse has fourteen legs, the velvet worm has several dozen, and the centipede has one pair of legs for each body segment which typically is fifty legs. But the winner with the most legs is (drum roll, please) the millipede. It has two pair of legs per body segment and can have anywhere between eighty and four hundred legs!

So that's a brief overview of locomotion. Before we move on (Get it, move on?), let us remember the reason for locomotion in the first place. Locomotion is designed to get us from here to there.

For Reflection/Discussion

- ✱ The most important question from this reflection, for humans at least, is this: Where am I going and why?
- ✱ Have you ever thought of locomotion as a special gift from God?

Your word is a lamp to my feet
and a light to my path.   ✱ PSALM 119:105

*Source of All Movement, direct my steps
ever closer to you.*

19 Rhinos, Warthogs, and Bats

Toads aren't ugly—they're just toads.

🐾 PROVERB WRITTEN BY A CHILD

What do these three animals have in common: rhinos, warthogs, and bats? If you said beauty and grace, you probably need glasses or you need *new* glasses. For the truth is, (I do not mean to offend here), these three animals all suffer from "beauty deficiency." In other words, they are all pretty ugly. I say that fully aware that beauty (and ugliness) is in the eye of the beholder. So a female rhino thinks a male rhino is pretty hot stuff, and visa-versa. But scientists have long known that rhinos have very poor eyesight, so that explains that.

In addition to their homeliness, rhinos, warthogs, and bats do not have a positive image. They do not elicit warm, fuzzy feelings in most people. Take the rhinoceros. His name is derived from two Greek words: *rhino* (nose) and *ceros* (horn). Most rhinos have a huge, ugly horn perched at the end of their nose. Some have two horns, as if one wasn't bad enough. Rhinos also weigh a couple of tons. Those horns coupled with all those pounds make rhinos a formidable foe. In fact, rhinos are one of the deadliest animals for humans, killing more people annually than even tigers and leopards. Needless to say, this fact does nothing to improve their image. Rhinos also have very thick skin (anywhere between 1.5 cm and 5 cm thick), which helps them to endure all the terrible things people say about them. One more interesting fact: a group of rhinos is called a "crash." It only makes sense.

Then there's the warthog. The warthog has four wart-like tusks on its head which contribute greatly to its beauty deficiency. Warthogs are much smaller than rhinos, weighing between 110 and 330 pounds and they are seemingly less testy. The males tend to live alone or in bachelor groups. The females and young live in larger groups called "sounders." The males join the females during mating season, assuring that there will be many new ugly warthogs born each year.

And finally, bats. The first thing that strikes me about bats is how many of them there are. Though relatively small animals, they account for twenty percent of all mammal species. Bats get a bad rap for spreading diseases. Yes, it is true they have a high tolerance for harboring pathogens and can spread diseases like rabies, but it is also true that they spread a lot of good things. Like pollen. In fact, many tropical plants are totally dependent on bats for their existence. Bats also spread the seeds of many plants all over the place via their excrement (in Greek, *poop*). Bats are beneficial also because of all the insects they devour—including mosquitoes that spread malaria.

The world of rhinos, warthogs, and bats reminds us that no one is totally ugly or totally beautiful, totally good or totally bad, totally innocent or totally guilty. It is the same way in the world of *homo sapiens*.

For Reflection/Discussion

- Which creatures in your opinion seem particularly unpleasant? What is their purpose in nature?
- Of whom or what do you need to be more understanding and accepting?

Beloved, let us love one another, because love is from God; everyone who loves is born of God and knows God.   ❦ 1 JOHN 4:7

God of All Creatures, give me
an understanding heart.

20 The Owl

I rejoice that there are owls.

✺ HENRY DAVID THOREAU

My first encounter with an owl was under circumstances less than ideal. One time on our farm, something started killing our geese. For several mornings when my father inspected his flock before going off to work, he found a dead goose or two. From the condition of the dead geese, he suspected they were being killed by an owl. My father had no recourse but to stop the owl from destroying his flock. So one day we herded all the geese into our coops and rain shelters for the night, while my father rigged a snare, using one dead goose as bait. The snare worked. The next morning there was a large reddish-brown barn owl in the trap.

I remember my mother taking me out early in the morning to see the owl close up. The dew was so heavy on the tall grass, she carried me. We stopped by the fence and gazed at the owl on the other side. It was still very much alive sitting in all its owlish dignity. I remember being mesmerized by the beauty of its plumage and its large yellow eyes. Instinctively I knew I was seeing something very, very special. That is one reason I can recall this incident with such clarity even though it happened over fifty-five years ago.

Over the years, I have had other encounters with owls under more favorable circumstances. I have spotted owls while hiking in the woods or while praying on retreat. Twice I have glimpsed them in winter, nestled in pine trees sound asleep. And many times I have heard their plaintive Whooo! Whooo! Whooo! while lying in bed at night.

Owls are found almost everywhere in the world except Antarctica and a few remote islands. Though they tend to be solitary, a group of owls is called a parliament. Somehow, that word seems fitting for them. Owls are nocturnal birds of prey. Part of the fascination of owls can be attributed to several of their physical characteristics. First, they possess large forward-facing eyes, a trait unusual for birds. In fact, only one other species of birds has this trait: penguins. The owl's eyes are further accented by a conspicuous circle of feathers called a facial disc. These feathers help funnel the sound of prey into the owl's ears. The owl's hearing is so acute, it can detect a mouse squeak a half a mile away.

Owls have become a symbol of wisdom in many cultures, a fact probably attributed to their almost human-like face. Strictly speaking, however, owls do not rate very high on the bird intelligence scale. Crows, jays, and magpies are smarter than owls. But owls do have excellent eyesight. They are far-sighted, however, so things are blurred for them if they are within a few inches of their eyes. Another remarkable characteristic of owls is their ability to turn their heads 270 degrees in both directions, thus enabling them to look over their own shoulders without turning their bodies. (You try looking over yours!) This ability aids them in their quest for food.

One of the most notable features of owls is the design of their feathers. Owl feathers, unlike the feathers of most other birds, have fluffy edges that muffle the sound of their wing beats. I once saw (maybe I should say I *heard*) this fact demonstrated when I visited a nature center in Colorado that cared for injured raptors. The guide held a large feather in each hand. He moved the first feather (a hawk's) up and down in the air and we heard a soft swishing sound. But when he moved the second one (an owl's) we heard nothing. Absolutely nothing. The flight of an owl is virtually silent. Their prey never hear them coming. Wildlife writer Warner Shedd calls owls "nature's original stealth aircraft."

Throughout history and in many parts of the world today, the owl is associated with death and misfortune. This association probably arises out of their nocturnal activities and their cries, which range from sadly melancholic to irritatingly screeching. In ancient mythology, owls were often companions for goddesses. In the story of King Arthur, Merlin's owl, named Archimedes, helped teach the young King

Arthur the way of the birds. More recently, Harry Potter had his companion owl, Hedwig.

When I think of the owl, I think of someone who owns the night. How *unlike* us humans, who tend to grope, falter, and make all kinds of noises as we stumble to find our way through the darkness. Owls, on the other hand, fly swiftly, surely, and silently through the forest at night. Both in day and night, owls are nearly cloaked in invisibility, making them hard to spot. Catching even a glimpse of one is pure gift.

For Reflection/Discussion

- Have you ever experienced an owl close up? What was most memorable about this encounter?
- What qualities of the owl do you find particularly interesting?

Again Jesus spoke to them, saying, "I am the light of the world. Whoever follows me will never walk in darkness but will have the light of life." ❧ John 8:12

*God of Wishes, help me to befriend
mystery and darkness.*

21 Photosynthesis Makes the World Go 'Round

I am very grateful for the color green.
If there had to be so much of anything,
best it be green.

❧ MIRIAM POLLARD, OCSO

*Y*ears ago my biology teacher at Notre Dame College in Cleveland, Ohio, was Sister Hubert. Though not known for her organizational skills or neatness, she was nonetheless a brilliant woman with a ready smile and deep devotion to biology. Sister instilled in her students a reverence for all living things. More than that, she found creative ways to help us learn and remember key biological phenomena.

I can still hear her say, "Young Ladies, today I am here

to tell you that it is not *love* that makes the world go round. It is photosynthesis!" And she proceeded to explain this incredible process that occurs in plants all over the planet, a process which few of us knew much about, let alone appreciated. Although I have long since forgotten the details of photosynthesis, I have never forgotten its supreme importance.

Essentially, photosynthesis is the process by which plants make their own food. The basic equation for photosynthesis is this: carbon dioxide + water + sunlight yields sugar and oxygen. Sugar becomes the plant's food while oxygen is given off as a waste product. This "waste product" is not really a waste. Plants help to keep oxygen at a healthy level in earth's atmosphere. Though photosynthesis was discovered in the 1800s, it is so complex that there are still some steps in the process we do not fully understand even today. But one thing we know for sure: photosynthesis is arguably the most important biochemical process known, because virtually all living things depend on it for their survival.

When we think of photosynthesis, we usually think of the color green. But this association is misleading. In a typical leaf, chlorophyll, the catalyst for photosynthesis, absorbs energy from the blue and red parts of the solar spectrum— which are the ends of the solar rainbow. The green middle of the spectrum is reflected, so that's the color we see with our eyes. "The leaf is green," we say. In reality, though, the colors used in photosynthesis are blue and red. Green is the color that's left over in the process.

Photosynthesis is Nature's Great Magic Show, a show which, in most plants, is largely performed by the leaves. A leaf might look like it is just sitting there doing nothing, but in actuality, it is very busy. Just peek at a live leaf under a microscope (as Sister Hubert had us do), and you will be amazed at all the bustling that is going on there. Every leaf is a teeny-weeny factory that is constantly manufacturing food to sustain the life of the plant. Plants never have to rely on other living things for their food—unlike all animals, including humans. (Okay, a few plants like the Venus Fly Trap do eat other organisms, but they are the exception, not the rule. In nature there are lots of rules, but also exceptions to those rules.)

Without photosynthesis, there would be no grass, trees, lettuce, or broccoli (obviously). But there would also be no beetles, trout, robins, chickens, cows, lions, monkeys, or humans. That's because virtually all living things depend on plants for the sugar that sustains their bodies. We humans, like many other animals, must get this sugar either directly from plants ("Eat your spinach!") or from the flesh of creatures that eat the plants ("Eat your hamburger!").

Humans need photosynthesis for other reasons besides food. We use the products of photosynthesis for fuel (wood and coal, for example), building materials (wood and thatch), and fiber (cotton and ramie). Scientists estimate that we humans use between one-third and one-half of all the products of photosynthesis. This is cause for concern. In some places, humans are destroying forests at an alarming rate. Satellite photos show that we are cutting down a part of the tropical forest the size of West Virginia annually. Such destruction can have devastating consequences for the entire world.

Through photosynthesis, plants help to maintain the balance of carbon dioxide in the atmosphere. Carbon dioxide, which is used in photosynthesis, traps heat from the sun resulting in the so-called "greenhouse effect." If the total number of plants is greatly reduced (through deforestation, for example), the level of carbon dioxide will rise significantly, thus contributing to global warming.

Sister Hubert's lessons on photosynthesis altered the way I looked at the plant world. She instilled in me a greater appreciation for all trees, bushes, shrubs, flowers, grasses, saplings, herbs, vines, weeds, shoots, and sprouts. She led me to reverence the magical power in a single leaf. And she taught me to see and appreciate the vital link between a single green leaf and the survival of life on Planet Earth.

For Reflection/Discussion

- ❧ Have you ever spent time thinking about/praying about photosynthesis?
- ❧ How can you give thanks for the gift of photosynthesis today?

Then God said, "Let the earth put forth vegetation: plants yielding seed, and fruit trees of every kind on earth that bear fruit with the seed in it." And it was so.

❧ GENESIS 1:11

*Creator of All Processes,
help me to reverence
all we already know about your
wonderful world, and all we have
yet to discover.*

22 The Mushroom Hunter

Sabbath is more than the absence of work....It is the presence of something that arises when we consecrate a period of time to listen to what is most deeply beautiful, nourishing, and true,...honoring those quiet forces of grace or spirit that sustain and heal us.

🍂 WAYNE MULLER

I remember Sunday mornings when I was a child. After church, I would sometimes see my father with his old shoes on (or sometimes even boots) and with a large basket in his hand, heading toward the woods across the road. Immediately I knew what he was up to. He was going mushroom hunting. I recall going with him only a few times. As a child I did not care much for mushrooms, so picking them did not interest me. Besides, although my father always welcomed us to come along with him, he never seemed to mind going alone. Looking back, I believe his long walks in the woods looking for mushrooms were special moments for Dad, his contemplative celebration of the Sabbath. After all, the other six days of the week, he was bent over a lathe in some dark, cramped machine shop, often for ten hours a day. This Sunday morning stroll in the woods must have nourished his soul.

An hour or two after my father had gone into the woods, he would emerge again often with his basket overflowing with mushrooms. If he had a good hunt, he could barely contain his excitement as he showed my mother his find: horse pinkies, hen-of-the-woods, stumpies. My mother shared his enthusiasm for mushrooms and always seemed happy to clean and prepare them for Dad just the way he liked them.

My father knew a lot about mushrooms. On the bookshelves in our living room were a number of mushroom books—some in English, others in Czech. Over the years my father became acquainted with scores of mushrooms, memorizing their names in three languages: English, Czech, and Latin. He was a good mushroom hunter because he knew where to look for different kinds of mushrooms: under a particular tree, near the creek, in the pine forest, out in a meadow. Sometimes people ask me, "Weren't you afraid of eating poison mushrooms?" These people know that some mushrooms (like the beautiful pure white mushroom called Angel of Death) are extremely poisonous and have no known antidote. As a family, though,

we never worried about eating poisonous mushrooms, because our Dad knew mushrooms too well.

The last year of Dad's life, he found it increasingly difficult
to walk. Shortly before his death, he confided to my mother
that one of the hardest things for him to accept was the fact
that he could not go mushroom hunting anymore.

We all need Sabbath moments in our lives, those times
when we engage in simple activities that bring us joy and
satisfaction, wrap us in solitude, and remind us of our deep
connectedness to all of creation—and to its Creator. For my
father, mushroom hunting was such an activity.

For Reflection/Discussion

- Have you ever been mushroom hunting? Or spent time
  alone in the woods?
- What are some of the Sabbath activities in your life?

Remember the Sabbath day, and keep it holy. For six
days you shall labor and do all your work. But the sev-
enth day is a Sabbath to the Lord your God....

 EXODUS 20:8–10

Loving God, teach me to create and celebrate
special Sabbath moments in my life.

23 Soil

Fresh-plowed ground has a subtle fra-grance. The dead of millions of years are in the earth, all the beasts and flying things, all the grasses, trees, bushes, all the bits and pieces of former lives.

❧ JUSTIN ISHERWOOD

My nephew Chris, who works in water conservation, is something of an environmentalist. He has taught me never to refer to the ground as *dirt*. Instead, always say *soil*. Why? Because the word *dirt* has a negative connotation implying worthlessness or even filth. But the word *soil* is more positive, connoting richness, nourishment, life.

Ever since I was a child, I have loved the soil. In early spring, I used to go into the garden right after the first plowing. I loved to walk in the deep-cut furrows—before my father or brothers did the disking. Following the example of my father, I used to reach down and pick up a clump of earth, smell its rich aroma, and crumble it in my hands. The experience was invigorating. Even the occasional worm or bug couldn't dampen the exhilaration I felt!

In his book *Wisconsin Trails and Tales,* Justin Isherwood writes beautifully about plowing. He calls plowing "a primitive art, a country square dance in which the farmer swings his earthy partner." As quoted above, he says this about the richness of soil: "The dead of millions of years are in the earth, all the beasts and flying things, all the grasses, trees, and bushes, all the bits and pieces of former lives." But the soil is much more than a massive grave. It is also the womb of new life. It is, in Isherwood's words, "the humble temple of life and civilization."

Naturalist Wendell Berry goes even further. He compares topsoil to Jesus himself. Berry says topsoil is Christ-like in its "passivity and beneficence and in the penetrating energy that issues out of its peaceableness." Topsoil "keeps the past, not as history or memory, but as richness, as new possibility."

For Reflection/Discussion

- How do you reverence the soil of the earth?
- Is there anything that has to die in you in order to bring forth new life?
- Do you keep the past as mere history or as richness and new possibility?

Then the Lord God formed man from the dust of the ground, and breathed into his nostrils the breath of life; and the man became a living being.

　　　　　　　　　　　　　　　　 GENESIS 2:7

God of New Possibility, teach me to reverence
the gift of soil today, the soil of the earth
as well as the soil of my soul.

24 The Pine Grove

The wilderness is near as well as dear to every man....The very uprightness of the pines and maples asserts the ancient rectitude and vigor of nature. Our lives need the relief of such a background, where the pine flourishes and the jay still screams.

🐿 HENRY DAVID THOREAU

*I*n 1958 the U.S. government gave my community, the Sisters of Notre Dame, three thousand pine trees to plant on our provincial center property in Chardon, Ohio. Our workmen, headed by August Siemer, painstakingly planted all those trees. In 1972, the government gave us an additional two thousand Canadian pines. Once again our workmen, this time led by Otto Hanish, planted those trees near where the other pines had been planted. Today, many years later, thousands of those pine trees survive, forming a beautiful pine grove that spreads across several acres of our land. These trees are very beneficial. They emit oxygen into the air, prevent erosion, provide shelter for deer, and are home to birds and burrowing creatures of all kinds. They are also simply beautiful to behold. Recently, I saw the impact of their beauty upon three of my grandnephews.

For several months my invalid mother resided in the health care center on our provincial house property where she had a view of the pine grove from her room. One day my sister and niece came to visit her bringing along my three grandnephews ages ten, eight, and six. It rained most of the afternoon, and I sensed the boys were getting a little restless. So when I saw a break in the clouds, I asked them if they wanted to go outside and see our pine grove, while their mother and grandma visited with great-grandma. "YES!" they cried in unison. So we put on our jackets and headed outside.

The pine grove is one of my favorite places on our property. When I step into it, I feel I am entering a magnificent temple or cathedral. It is always very peaceful and quiet there, even on the windiest days. As I walk among the trees, I cannot even hear my own footsteps because the carpet of pine needles is so thick. I knew the boys liked nature, but I was not too sure if they would appreciate this "holy place."

But as soon as we entered the grove, I saw their eyes get really big. Zachary, the middle boy, was the first to speak. "WOW!" he said. "WOW!" as he turned himself slowly around and around, gazing in wonder at all the trees. "This is so beautiful!" he cried. And to make sure I heard him, he cried again, "This is soooooo beautiful!"

Aaron, the oldest, was also taken by the beauty of the grove, as was Cameron, the youngest. Aaron asked, "Has Grandma ever seen this place?" Before I could answer, he added, "Because she would reeeeeally love it!" Then Zachary asked, "Has Mom ever seen this?" I said I did not think she ever had. He asked, "Can we bring her and Grandma here to see it?" I assured them we could. I was happy to see that their response to the beauty of the grove included the desire to share it with someone else.

We spent several minutes in the pine grove examining the carpet of needles, the few fallen trees, the many snake and groundhog holes, and the array of mushrooms sprouting up here and there. As we left the pine grove, I told them, "Next time you come, I'll take you to the woods to see our giant oak tree." They were excited at the prospect.

Later that night, I thanked God that these three young boys were so appreciative of the beauty of the pine grove. I thanked God that their parents and grandparents have instilled in them a basic love for nature, one of the most precious legacies they will ever receive.

For Reflection/Discussion

- From whom did you get your love for nature?
- How are you passing on this legacy of love to the children in your life?

Praise the name of the Lord;
you that stand in the house of the Lord,
in the courts of the house of our God.

 PSALM 135:1, 2

God of the Pine Grove,
you are my shelter and home.

25 Miracles: Our Daily Bread

Miracles seem to me to rest not so much upon faces or voices or healing power coming suddenly from far off, but upon our perceptions being made finer, so that for a moment our eyes can see and our ears hear what is about us always.

🐾 WILLA CATHER

*W*hen something extraordinary happens, we call it a miracle. A blind person suddenly sees. A brain tumor mysteriously disappears. A woman, told she can never have a child, becomes pregnant.

But there is a miracle more fundamental than any of these extraordinary happenings. It is the miracle that *anything exists at all—and keeps on existing.* Stars, rocks, water, fire. And the most miraculous of existing things is life itself. Writer Wendell Berry says it well: That anything exists—be it lilies or sparrows—"in this warm world within the cold and empty stellar distances" is miraculous. He goes on to say that "the miraculous is not the extraordinary but the common mode of existence. It is our daily bread." Berry calls Jesus' turning of the water into wine "a very small miracle." And adds, "We forget the greater and still continuing miracle by which water (and soil and sunlight) is turned into grapes."

In the public ministry of Jesus there is a discernible movement in his working of miracles. Throughout the gospels, Jesus performs extraordinary deeds. He feeds a crowd of five thousand with a few loaves of bread and a couple of fish. He cures a paralytic. He raises Lazarus back to life. These occurrences show there is a place in our faith for miracles, that is, for the surprisingly wonderful.

But if we examine the public ministry of Jesus more closely, we notice that as time went on, these kinds of miracles became fewer and fewer. Toward the end of his life, at least in the synoptic gospels, Jesus performs very few miracles. In Gethsemane, Jesus begs his Father, Abba, for a miracle: "Father, if you are willing, remove this cup from me" (Lk 22:42). In other words, work a miracle so I will not have to die this awful death. Then Jesus adds, "Not my will, but yours be done." Jesus does not get the miracle for which he prays so passionately. He is arrested, tried, and executed. But the far greater miracle was his acceptance of his passion and death, an acceptance made possible by the miracle of faith.

When the soldiers seize Jesus and bind him, he offers no resistance. In Luke's account, one of the disciples clumsily tries to defend Jesus with his sword and ends up cutting off the ear of the High Priest's servant. The only miracle Jesus works in Gethsemane is to heal that man's ear. While Jesus hangs dying on the cross, bystanders taunt him, telling him to climb down off the cross and save himself. But Jesus does not do this. Instead he asks his Father to forgive those who kill him (talk about a miracle!) and then commends his spirit into the Father's hands.

It all boils down to this: What constitutes a miracle? A maple tree that stays green all year long or a maple tree whose leaves turn a brilliant red and orange each autumn before falling to the ground? A sun that dances wildly in the sky or a sun that rises each morning and sets each evening? Being able to walk on water or having fresh, clean water every day to drink? Being cured of painful arthritis or being able to live with arthritis and still be a cheerful, caring person? Being healed of lung cancer or being able to face death with equanimity and total trust in God?

Sometimes the ordinary is extraordinary. Sometimes the miraculous is the everyday.

For Reflection/Discussion

- 🐦 What is your reaction to Willa Cather's statement at the beginning of this reflection?
- 🐦 What are some of the ordinary miracles in your everyday life?

Then Jesus said to him, "Unless you see signs and wonders you will not believe." The official said to him, "Sir, come down before my little boy dies." Jesus said to him, "Go; your son will live." The man believed the word that Jesus spoke to him and started on his way. As he was going down, his slaves met him and told him that his child was alive.   🐦 JOHN 4:48–51

Loving God, give me a greater appreciation
of the ordinary miracles in my daily life.

26 Snakes

To the poet, to the philosopher, to the
saint, all things are friendly and sacred,
all events are profitable, all days are
holy, all people are divine.

🎵 RALPH WALDO EMERSON

Snakes have a bad press. Just yell "snake!" at a family picnic and see what happens. Most people will scream "Eeeeek!" and run away. It is unfortunate that snakes are so feared and even hated by so many people, for scientists tell us snakes hold a very important place in the eco-system. By eating bugs, rodents, and other animals, snakes are a vital link in the great food chain. My father, for one, was always happy to see a garter snake slithering in his garden.

"But snakes bite!" someone might argue. Yes, they can bite, but most snakes will not attack humans unless startled or injured. In fact, the vast majority of snakes go to great lengths to avoid all contact with humans. (I guess humans have a bad press with snakes!)

"But some snakes are poisonous!" one could say. Strictly speaking, no snake is poisonous, but some species are venomous. Some frogs are poisonous. Just touch them and you could die. But snakes are venomous, which means they must inject their prey or enemy with venom to do any harm. In the wide array of snakes, relatively few are venomous. Of the ones that are, even fewer possess venom powerful enough to kill a human being. It is a documented fact that far more people in the United States are killed annually by lightning than by snakes.

Others will argue, "But snakes are so sneaky the way they slither on the ground." Yes, they do slither, but that is simply because they have no legs. Are snakes sneaky? They are no sneakier, let us say, than a swan. And swans are known for aggressively attacking humans especially during the nesting season. And swans can bite too!

Some people hate snakes because, "They're slimy." But I can tell you from first-hand experience that snakes are not slimy. At least the big kind I touched one day. It happened at one of the high schools where I taught. A boy came to a soccer game after school one time with a large brown and white snake curled on top of his head like a turban. Needless to say, he attracted quite a bit of attention—or at least the snake did. Also needless to say, the snake's arrival caused a large segment of the crowd to scatter! The boy invited me to touch his snake. I did. Albeit gingerly. And I can attest: That snake was not slimy.

The snake's image got no support from the author of Genesis either. Playing on our basic aversion to snakes, the author made the tempter in the Garden of Eden a snake. He might have helped the snakes' public image if he had made the tempter some other creature—like a beagle puppy perhaps. (It is easier for me to imagine Eve dialoguing with a puppy than with a snake!)

When it comes to snakes and other creatures that I might have a hard time warming up to, I always recall my mother's wise words, "Oh well, they're God's creatures too!" She said this of the squirrels who regularly stole the sunflower seeds from her bird feeder, but I think it applies to snakes and other creatures as well.

For Reflection/Discussion

- What is your attitude toward snakes?
- Are there any creatures in the world you fear or loathe? Why?

"See, I am sending you out like sheep into the midst of wolves; so be wise as serpents and innocent as doves."

 MATTHEW 10:16

*Lover of All, help me be more open to
all your creatures (including some humans
I know) who suffer from a bad press.*

27 Mountains

They are sacred and majestic mountains, ominous, enormous, noble, stirring. You want to attend to them. I could not keep my eyes off them.
 ❧ THOMAS MERTON

Mountains cover 24% of the earth's land mass and play a critical role in supporting the life of the planet. Virtually all the world's major rivers are fed from mountain sources. More than half the world's population depend on mountains for their water. Mountains cover 54% of Asia, 36% of North America, 25% of Europe, 22% of South America, 17% of Australia, and 3% of Africa.

The highest mountains are found in the Himalayas where the average mountain rises five kilometers above sea level. There is an exclusive club of fourteen mountains called "the eight-thousanders," which are all over eight thousand meters high. All of these mountains are in Asia. The Andes Mountains of South America are the next highest mountains with an average height of four kilometers. But the Andes are much younger mountains than the Himalayas. They are growing significantly higher every year and will eventually be taller than the Himalayas. Most other mountain ranges in the world average between 2 and 2.5 kilometers. Mt. Everest is earth's highest mountain, jutting 8,848 meters or 29,029 feet into the air.

It is interesting to note that in past ages there were mountains much taller than Everest on earth—some as high as twelve thousand meters—located in the Canadian Shield, a huge area of land that runs north from the Great Lakes all the way to the Arctic Circle. But even mountains do not stay the same forever, and these ancient Canadian mountains are now rolling hills. Similarly the Appalachian Mountains in the eastern United States were at one time taller than the Rockies.

When does a hill become a mountain? There is no consensus, but many people accept the English standard, which says a mountain is any land over six hundred meters (two thousand feet).

Humans have always been fascinated with mountains. For the most part, however, mountains have not been too friendly to humans. Some mountains (volcanoes) spew fire, sulfur, and molten rock. Wise humans give such mountains wide berth. High mountains also do not support agriculture, an industry we humans rely on for our very survival. In addition, mountains provide less oxygen for human habitation and more exposure to harmful solar radiation. But mountains' general lack of friendliness toward humans has not deterred people from exploring them. Moutaineering (called alpinism in Europe) is a popular sport, hobby, and even profession for some individuals. In recent years, the rise in popularity of skiing, snow boarding, and mountain climbing attests to the mountain's lure.

In ancient times, mountains were often associated with the gods. The Greeks believed Zeus and his gang of gods lived on Mt. Olympus. In other religions, mountaintops became favorite places to encounter one's deity. Moses trekked up Mt. Sinai to converse with Yahweh. Jesus liked mountains too. Mountains were one of his favorite places to pray. In the gospel of Matthew we read: "(Jesus) went up the mountain by himself to pray. When evening came, he was there alone" (Mt 14:23). Jesus also experienced the transfiguration on Mt. Tabor and the agony in the garden on the Mt. of Olives.

Poets like Dante and St. John of the Cross viewed mountains as images of our spiritual journey. St. John called his book *The Ascent of Mount Carmel.* He and other mystics likened the path to God to climbing a mountain.

In her beautiful book, *Pilgrim at Tinker Creek*, Annie Dillard describes both our fascination with mountaintops and our fear of them. She writes, "I have never understood why so many mystics of all creeds experience the presence of God on mountaintops. Aren't they afraid of being blown away?" She continues, "It often feels best to lie low, inconspicuous, instead of waving your spirit around from high places like a lightning rod." Dillard implies that only the truly holy or the truly foolish risk such an unprotected encounter with God. The rest of us take shelter "in a curved, hollow place" where we are "vulnerable to only a relatively narrow column of God as air."

For Reflection/Discussion

- Have you ever experienced any mountains? In what ways?
- How do mountains speak to your spiritual life?

"Come, let us go up to the mountain of the Lord...."

Isaiah 2:3

Maker of Mountains, give me the strength and courage to continue my climb to you.

28 Water

Water is a lot like God.

> ✿ Karol A. Jackowski

ecently, my religious community took a corporate stance with regard to water. Our statement summarized what we intended to do. We began by affirming that "water is a basic right for life." We promised personally to "reverence water as a sacred gift." More specifically, we pledged "to protect the waters entrusted to us" and to act to ensure the right to water "for all, especially the poor in areas where our Sisters serve." For one entire year we studied, discussed, and prayed about water. Then we took several specific action steps that grew out of our discussion and prayer.

Viewed from space, Planet Earth is truly "the blue water planet." Water covers 71% of Earth's surface and is found in many forms: oceans, ice caps, clouds, rain water, rivers, fresh water aquifers (underground reservoirs), lakes, and sea ice. Water is truly a gift, absolutely essential for all known life forms. It is a mystery too. Though colorless in small amounts, water is blue in larger quantities. Water continuously moves through a cycle of evaporation, precipitation, and runoff to the sea. As it does, it changes into different states: liquid, solid, and gas.

Water is a purifier in most religions including Hinduism, Judaism, Christianity, Islam, and Shinto. Many faiths hold particular sources of water as sacred, for example, the River Ganges in Hinduism, Lourdes in Christianity, and the Zamzam Well in Islam.

Water is the seed of life. Without it, all life would die. Though we humans can live without food for more than a month, we can live without water for only a week. Yet day by day we barely give water a second thought. What a contrast to the people of the Old Testament who lived in arid lands. They linked the precious gift of water to God's generous bounty. Throughout the psalms, for example, water is praised, valued, and celebrated. The psalmist says, "You make springs gush forth in the valleys; they flow between the hills, giving drink to every wild animal; the wild asses quench their thirst" (104:10–11). Psalm 42 links the thirst for water to our thirst for God: "As a deer longs for flowing streams, so my soul longs for you, O God" (verse 1). The Israelites also recalled how God held back the waters of the Red Sea for them as they fled the Egyptians (Ex 14). And later, how God held back the waters of the Jordan to allow Joshua to lead the people across with the Ark of the Covenant (Jos 3).

The basic right to water is being threatened today by several factors. First, its scarcity. Though water is plentiful on Earth, less than 3% of it is freshwater and thus drinkable. And over 2% of Earth's freshwater is frozen in glaciers and ice caps. This leaves less than 1% of all the water on Earth for human agriculture, industries, and communities. The right to water is also threatened by inequities in its use. Each American uses 153 gallons of water per day, each Briton 88 gallons, each Asian 23 gallons, and each African 12 gallons. In some places just collecting enough water for drinking, cooking, and personal hygiene is a major project Hauling heavy containers of water from a distant source can take several hours a day for some families. The task of carrying water almost always falls to girls and women.

Another major threat concerning water is the increased privatization of water. In some places, private companies are laying claim to water sources for manufacturing purposes, thus depriving the surrounding community of their basic human right to water. The document *Water, An Essential Element for Life,* by the Pontifical Council for Justice and Peace, says this: "Water cannot be treated as a mere product of consumption among others since it has an inestimable and irreplaceable value."

I never appreciated water more than when I visited our Sisters in Uganda. Water is so scarce there that the Sisters have to collect rain water into large storage tanks from the roofs of their school and convent. Each Saturday morning, one of the Sisters boils all the drinking water for the week. Needless to say, I never wasted a drop of water the whole time I was there. And I pretty much continued this practice of conserving water even when I returned back to the States.

For Reflection/Discussion

- Have you ever reflected on the value of water and its uses?
- How can you reverence and conserve water today?

Jesus said to her, "Everyone who drinks of this water will be thirsty again, but those who drink of the water that I will give them will never be thirsty. The water that I will give will become in them a spring of water gushing up to eternal life." JOHN 4:13–14

Creator, Redeemer, Sanctifier, give me a greater reverence for water and keep me mindful of the need to share this blessing with all peoples.

29 The Heart

Listen to your life. See it for the fathom-
less mystery that it is....Touch, taste,
smell your way to the holy and hidden
heart of it, because in the last analysis,
all moments are key moments and life
itself is grace.

🐦 FREDERICK BUECHNER

When I was a sophomore in high school, my friend Kay and I worked on a science project together. We put a dozen or so chicken eggs in an incubator that my brother John had made for us out of a wooden box, light bulb, and thermostat. For four weeks, we charted the development of the embryo into a fluffy baby chick. This meant we periodically removed an egg from the incubator, cracked it open, and noted what we observed.

This task was not easy for two fifteen-year-old girls—especially when the embryo began to resemble a baby chick. But I will always remember the day we saw the beating heart for the first time. There, in the midst of this pinkish blob, was a tiny reddish dot—no bigger than the little "o" in the word "dot." And it was beating—tha-thump, tha-thump, tha-thump. We gazed in awe as it continued to beat for several minutes. Later we dutifully noted the time in our journal. Because of that experience, I can appreciate how parents must feel when they hear and see for the first time the beating heart of their unborn child. "Tha-thump, tha-thump, tha-thump," it says. "I am here; I am alive; I am coming."

Of all the organs in the human body, the heart tends to arouse the most wonder. Once it starts beating, it continues to do so with never a break until death. (Unless, of course, you have a heart attack or you are put on a heart machine during surgery.) We recently buried a Sister who was 104. Can you imagine how many times her heart beat in her lifetime?

Centuries ago we humans designated the heart as the source of love. Biologically speaking that is not accurate, of course, but it is romantic. We even give so-called "heart shaped" valentines to one another in February. Again, valentines are not really heart shaped, but long ago we opted for symmetrical beauty rather than anatomical truth.

The Bible is filled with hundreds of references to the heart, many of them supporting the view of the heart as the locus of love. Some of my favorite references are from the psalms: "You have put gladness in my heart more than when their grain and wine abound" (Ps 4:7). "The precepts of the Lord are right, rejoicing the heart" (Ps 19:8). "Be strong, and let your heart take courage, all you who wait for the Lord" (Ps 31:24). "Create in me a clean heart, O God" (Ps 51:10). "Search me, O God, and know my heart" (Ps 139:23).

And who of us can forget these immortal words of Jesus? "Learn from me; for I am gentle and humble in heart" (Mt 11:29). Today might be a good day to take a few minutes to pay attention to the beating of your heart. Simply put two fingers on your jugular vein or wrist and feel the rhythmic pulsing of your heart for a few minutes. What do you think or feel as you do this?

For Reflection/Discussion

- 🌺 Do you ever "listen to your life"? In what particular ways?
- 🌺 What effect can the awareness of your heart beat have on you and your prayer?

"For the Lord does not see as mortals see; they look on the outward appearance, but the Lord looks on the heart." 🌺 1 SAMUEL 16:7

Create in me a loving heart, O God.

30 The Fruit and Berry Chart

Truth is given to us daily, harvested
from the fields of our own experience.
🍎 MELANNIE SVOBODA, SND

My father used to have a fruit and berry chart. Sent to him by some seed company, it charted the harvest time for dozens of fruits and berries that grow in our particular climate zone. What amazed me about the chart was how the various fruits and berries were staggered across the page. The first to come are the strawberries. They are followed a few weeks later by raspberries and blueberries. Next come blackberries and lastly the elderberries. The fruits do not come all at once either. Plums and pears make their appearance first, followed later by apples and grapes.

It is as if the Grand Designer of Fruit and Berries had intentionally planned things this way, realizing it would not be good for Earth's animals if all fruits and berries ripened at the same time. If they all ripened in June, for example, Earth's animals would be inundated with food, with much of it going to waste. And then these same animals would have nothing to eat in July, August, and September. No, thought the Grand Designer, better to have each fruit and berry ripen in its own time (with a little overlapping), thus insuring there will be fruit and berries all summer long and into the fall.

In the Our Father we pray, "Give us this day our daily bread." The operative word is *daily*. God is not an all-at-once sort of person. Rather God seems to give us what we need for today, calling us to trust that we will be given what we need for tomorrow. When I am tempted to want it all—and now!—I recall the fruit and berry chart. First come the strawberries, I say to myself. Be patient. The apples and grapes will come in their own due time.

For Reflection/Discussion

- ❧ Are you sometimes impatient with nature's cycles? How do you deal with this?
- ❧ How does God give you your *daily* bread?

Surely goodness and mercy shall follow me
all the days of my life....   ❧ PSALM 23:6

*Grand Designer of All, help me to trust you
to give me what I need today and every day.*

31 How Much Time Do You Have?

*I still find each day too short for all the
thoughts I want to think, all the walks
I want to take, all the books I want to
read, and all the friends I want to see.*

❧ John Burroughs

A study of nature reveals that various life forms have
different life expectancies. A mouse can expect to
live four years, a rabbit nine, a pigeon twenty-six,
a deer thirty-five, a crocodile forty-five, and an elephant sev-
enty. The oldest chimpanzee, Cheeta, is seventy-four. Notice
I used the verb *is* because, at this writing, he is still alive. You
might remember Cheeta (if you're old enough), because he
starred in many Hollywood Tarzan movies. Other animals
fare even better than Cheeta. In recent years, bowhead whales
have been found with harpoons in their bodies dating back

to the 1800s. One such whale, after an autopsy, was determined to be 211 years old.

Then there's the Aldabra giant tortoises. Although these animals were thought to live beyond one hundred years, it was hard to verify their exact age because they outlived their human observers. But researchers generally agree that the oldest documented tortoise, named Adwaitya, died in 2006 at the age of 255.

A few members of the plant world live even longer than us animals. A certain bristlecone pine tree, appropriately named Methuselah, lives somewhere in the White Mountains of California. Scientists say it is 4,770 years old, the oldest living single organism ever documented. The tree sits in an undisclosed location to protect it against human vandals, who, in a raging fit of jealousy I suppose, might try to kill it.

Most insects seem to get shortchanged when it comes to long lives. A worker bee lives only one year; a worker ant lives only one-half a year. (Worker ants must have a weaker union). Some species of moths live for a mere twenty-four hours. You will never hear these moths say *mañana;* for them there is only *hoy.*

Where do we humans fall on the life expectancy scale? The average life expectancy for the world population is sixty-six, but that number is deceptive. Life expectancy for humans varies greatly from country to country. An American can expect to live 77.7 years. But a Mozambican has a life expectancy of only 40.3 years. Spain has the highest life-expectancy at

82.3. Other so-called third-world countries fare even worse than Mozambique. This means we can never take credit for our longevity, which is largely determined by which country our parents happened to live in.

The oldest documented human being was Jeanne Calmet of Arles, France, who lived to be 122 years and 164 days old. She was amazingly active, taking up fencing at eighty-five and still riding her bike at 100. In 1965, when she was a mere ninety, she signed a contract with a lawyer, Francois Raffray, age forty-seven. Called a "reverse mortgage," the contract stipulated that Raffray would pay Calmet a monthly sum of money for her apartment. Upon her death, Raffray would get the apartment regardless of how much he had paid her. At the time they signed the contract, Calmet's apartment was valued at ten years of monthly payments. Since she was already ninety, Raffray thought he had made a great deal. But he was greatly mistaken. He ended up paying Calmet every month for thirty years! When he himself died of cancer at age seventy-seven, his poor widow had to continue to make the payments until Calmet's death in 1997.

There's an old poem that speaks of the length of one's life in a unique way. It describes how the dates on a tombstone are often separated by a dash. The poet muses that the dash represents all the time the person lived on earth. We never know how short or long our dash will be. What matters in the end, he says, are not the dates on the tombstone. What matters, is how we lived our dash. He concludes:

For it matters not how much we own—
    the cars, the house, the cash.
What matters is how we live and love and
    how we spend our dash.

For Reflection/Discussion

- In what ways do you express appreciation for your gift of life?
- How will you spend your dash today?

So teach us to count our days
that we may gain a wise heart.   PSALM 90:12

Author of Life, help me to
treasure the time I have.

32 The Pith of a Feather

The door to God, the door to any grace is very little, very ordinary.

✿ JESSICA POWERS

*O*ne thing that fascinates me is the way scientists name things. They don't call things by the same names we do—like dandelion, maple tree, robin, termite, or squirrel. No, scientists use names like *taraxacum* (dandelion), *acer saccharinum* (maple tree), *turdus migratorius)* robin, *isoptera* (termite), and *sciurus carolinensis* (squirrel). Scientists tend to speak in Latin—probably to show how smart they are. You can do the same thing. The next time you are out walking with friends and you see a robin, impress them by yelling, "Look, there's a *turdus migratorius!*"

Even things that do not breathe or move get fancy names. Rocks get names like *cataclasite, granodiorite,* and *nepheline syenite*. I have seen pictures of these rocks and they all look like rocks to me. Sometimes scientists run out of names (there are only so many letters in the Latin alphabet), so they have to use numbers to name things. Astronomers do this all the time due to the vastness of the universe. You try to come up with names for all the stars when there are billions of galaxies in the universe, each containing as many as one trillion stars! So some stars have names like Castor, Izar, and Polaris, but many more have numbers like these: HD 128621, GO51-015, V645, LHS 138. I know, they look like flight confirmation numbers, but they really are the names of stars.

Not content with giving names or numbers to virtually everything in the known universe, scientists like to give names to *parts* of things too. This comes from their habit of looking so closely at things. Take a feather. Most of us, upon spotting a feather on the ground would look down at it and think, "Some poor bird has lost a feather," and walk on. But not the scientist. He (or she) will stop, pick up the feather, and carry it back very carefully to the laboratory in a plastic bag. Once there he (or she) will examine it—first with the naked eye, noting its color, size, texture, temperature, and a hundred other things most of us could not even imagine. By doing this, the scientist will then determine what kind of bird the feather came from and from which part of the bird's body. He (or she) will even tell you how old the bird was, what it ate for lunch, and what state of mind it was in when it lost the feather. Then the scientist will put the feather under a microscope and see that the feather has *parts*. And he will proceed to name the parts: barb, down, shaft, opening at the end of the shaft, and pith. All of this—for a feather!

It reminds me of a story by John Updike called "Pigeon Feathers" in which a young boy, David, ends up shooting some pesky pigeons on the farm. Most people consider pigeons nothing but a nuisance—and a dirty one at that. Some people show their contempt for pigeons by calling them "sky rats." Anyway, David goes to bury one of the dirty dead pigeons and he suddenly notices its feathers. He stops and examines them more closely and thinks how beautiful they are, how intricate, how perfectly formed! In short, David is eventually led to a belief in God just by contemplating the complexity and intricacy of those pigeon feathers.

Anyone who has ever looked closely at even the pith of a feather can understand why.

For Reflection/Discussion

- In what ways do you show reverence for the "little things" of life?
- What might you look at more closely today?

O that I had wings like a dove!
I would fly away and be at rest....   🍂 PSALM 55:6

*God Beyond All Naming, help me to
contemplate your intricate designs everywhere—
even in the pith of my everyday life.*

33 The Buck Stopped Here

There are voiceless insights to be gleaned from the species that surround us if only we would stop and be with them.

🖙 F. Lynne Bachleda

When I lived in Middleburg, I often took walks in the woods. The school sat on a 180-acre estate so there were plenty of woods for me to explore. One Friday afternoon after school, I went into the woods as I had done many times before. Sometimes on my walks, I would run across deer. But the deer were almost always do and our encounters were fleeting.

But on this particular day, as I hiked along one of the horse paths, my mind was on things other than seeing deer. As I trudged up a gentle hill and turned a bend in the path, I came face to face with a buck. He was beautiful. And he was big. So were his antlers. The wind must have been blowing toward me, which meant I was down wind from him. Evidently, he did not pick up my scent, for he just stood there, only about ten feet away, and stared at me. I stood motionless, trying not to blink or even take any noticeable breaths. I wanted the moment to last forever.

As we stood facing each other, I saw his nose twitch a few times, searching for my scent. He turned his large head to the side once or twice, as if trying to get a better look at me, or at least to view me from a slightly different angle. We stood there for several moments. Just the two of us. Human and animal. Woman and buck. Gazing into each other's eyes. Only afterwards did I feel a twinge of fear when I recalled those impressive antlers and sharp hooves. But during our encounter, my only feeling was awe. Unadulterated awe. In my mind, I found myself saying over and over to him, "You are magnificent! You are simply magnificent!"

The buck was the first to stir. After a few more moments, it became bored with me. He turned and started to walk away, pausing once or twice to check me out again. Then apparently satisfied that I was nothing to fear or pay much mind to, he trotted away. He did not run or leap; he just trotted—rather leisurely. I watched him as he disappeared into the thick foliage of the trees. Only after I could see or hear him no longer, did I take a deep breath, look up toward the canopy of trees and whisper aloud, "Thank you, God! Thank you! Thank you!"

I do not know much about working for peace, but I pray every day for those who do. I pray for negotiators of all kinds who devote themselves selflessly to bringing two "sides" together to talk, thus averting potential wars—from playground squabbles to armed global conflicts. I do not know if peace will ever come to some of the war-torn areas of our world. But if it is ever achieved, this I do know: It will begin with people meeting face to face. It will begin with people looking directly into the eyes of their enemy and seeing not hatred or malice or evil, but seeing a person like themselves—with fears and hopes and triumphs and failures and doubts and dreams—and in that meeting, both sides will experience anew the miracle and mystery they share together called life.

For Reflection/Discussion

- Have you ever had an encounter like Sr. Melannie's? What was your reaction?
- Is there anyone you need to meet face to face?

"I give you a new commandment, that you love one another. Just as I have loved you, you also should love one another." ✽ JOHN 13:34

God of Mystery, God of Miracles, help me to see my own hopes and fears in those I meet today.

34 What Do You Say?

Nothing in the world is single,
All things by a law divine
In each other's being mingle.

🐿 PERCY BYSSHE SHELLEY

*I*n nature's world there is a lot of talking going on. Perhaps talking is not the right word here if by talking I mean something we do with our mouths. It is more accurate to say that in nature's world there is a lot of communication going on, much of which we humans are only faintly aware.

Let's begin with the animals. The study of animal communication is called *zoosemiotics* to differentiate it from human communication which is called *anthroposemiotics*. The science of *zoosemiotics* divides animal communication into two parts: interspecies (between different species) and intraspecies (within the same species). Interspecies is often between predator and prey. Some creatures (who are small and therefore often fall into the prey category) communicate by color to their predators (who are often larger). The yellow-winged darter dragonfly, for example, is bright yellowish-orange. That color warns predators of its noxious quality. It is as if the dragonfly were wearing a red flashing sign on its back that said, "WARNING! DO NOT EAT ME! I AM POISONOUS!" Over the years, birds seem to have gotten the message and they leave the yellow-winged dragonfly alone.

Most interspecies communication, however, is from predator to prey. A wolf will growl and bare its teeth at its prey. A rattlesnake will rattle its rattle. A bull will snort, dig its front hooves into the dirt, and put its head down to showcase its massive horns. (Somehow these animals remind me of some humans I know.) Another prime example of interspecies communication is between humans and their pets. When you tell your dog to fetch or roll over, this is interspecies communication—unless your dog just sits there with a puzzled look on its face. Or if your dog sits by the door and barks and barks, telling you it needs to go outside, that is interspecies communication as well.

By far most animal communication is intraspecies. The most familiar is bird songs. The majority of bird singing is done by male birds, but in some species both sexes sing. In fact, some birds sing duets together as a way of strengthening their marital bond. Other examples of intraspecies communication include the warning cries of monkeys and the mating calls of frogs. Mating frogs are those "spring peepers" so many of us love to hear in early spring. (A friend of mine moved from Ohio to Utah. She confessed one of the things she missed the most was hearing those spring peepers!)

But animals use more than their mouths to communicate. There is a great deal of olfactory communication going on which we humans, with our very limited sense of smell, miss completely. Many mammals have specific glands that generate distinctive and long-lasting smells that they leave almost everywhere to mark their territory or to let other animals know of their presence. They sometimes also accomplish this marking with their urine or feces. (Even the human nose can usually detect this type of olfactory communication.) Mongolian gerbils have scent glands on their stomachs which they rub against objects, undeterred by how ridiculous they look when they are doing it. Felines have glands on their flanks or their cheeks. When your cat rubs itself against your legs, it is really marking you as its possession. (And you thought *you* owned the cat!) Bees carry with them a little pouch of material that releases a scent when they return to the hive. The scent tells all the other bees they belong to this particular hive. It is like using a passport to get back into your country. Bees also perform intricate dances that tell the other bees exactly where they found some good nectar. Evidently bees like to share their joy (and work load) with other bees.

Plants communicate as well. Let me give just one general example. The colorful and sweet-smelling blossoms of many flowers are designed not merely to delight humans. They are also the plant's way of inviting bees and other insects to stop in for some nectar and (in the process of visiting) to pollinate the plant, thus insuring the survival of that species into the future.

Communication, then, is vital in the lives of nature's creatures and plants. It aids in survival. It assures nourishment. It facilitates bonding. It bestows a sense of belonging. It shares vital information. If zoosemiotics does this for animals, imagine what *anthroposemiotics* can do for humans.

For Reflection/Discussion

- 🔖 What are some of the animal communications you have been aware of?
- 🔖 What are your communication strengths? What are some of your communication weaknesses?

Divided tongues, as of fire, appeared among them, and a tongue rested on each of them. All of them were filled with the Holy Spirit and began to speak in other languages, as the Spirit gave them ability.   🔖 ACTS 2:3–4

Origin of all Communication,
assist me with my words, signs,
and gestures today.

35 Snowflakes

Nature is full of genius, full of divinity;
so that not a snowflake escapes its fash-
ioning hand.

🍎 HENRY DAVID THOREAU

I live in Chardon, Ohio, about thirty miles east of Cleveland. Chardon lies in what is called the "snow belt." This means in winter we get something that meteorologists (a fancy name for weathermen but it also includes weatherwomen) refer to as "lake effect snow." Lake effect snow occurs when the wind, while blowing across Lake Erie, picks up moisture from the open water and manufactures massive quantities of snow, which it then dumps onto the snow belt. We in Chardon get much more snow than our neighbors. If our neighbors, for example, get one inch of snow, we get five. If they get three inches, we get fourteen. If they get ten, we get thirty-seven. There are two ways we Chardonites can react to getting buried under lake effect snow. We can complain about it. ("Darn it! It's snowing again!") Or we can brag about it. ("Ha! You think your twenty-four inches is a lot of snow? We have fifty-six inches here and it's still coming down!") Most native Chardonites have opted for the latter.

Living in the snow belt means we see a lot of snowflakes. Snowflakes are simply ice crystals formed thousands of feet above the earth that eventually make their way down to us, covering everything—roads, trees, bushes, houses, sidewalks, cars—with a blanket of white. That blanket is often a delight to behold, but a pain to shovel. Physicist Kenneth Libbrecht and photographer Patricia Rasmussen teamed up to produce a fascinating book about snowflakes entitled *The Snowflake: Winter's Beauty.* I don't know which of them had the greater challenge, Libbrecht who had to translate all those scientific explanations into language we non-scientists could understand, or Rasmussen who had to photograph all those little snowflakes while standing outside in the bitter cold!

The book is filled with gorgeous pictures of real snowflakes. (I take that back. Not all are *real* snowflakes. A few of the flakes are "artificial," that is, made by a snow machine at some ski resort. They are not nearly as pretty as the real snowflakes.) The book also shares many facts about snowflakes. In the Middle Ages, for example, scientists were so amazed at the remarkable symmetry of snowflakes that they wondered if snowflakes had souls. Henry David Thoreau writing in his journal in 1856 says this about snowflakes: "I should hardly admire them more if real stars fell and lodged on my coat."

The book also points out that snowflakes come in a variety of shapes. They can be symmetrical or asymmetrical, stellar or columnar, needles or bullets. Altogether there are now eighty classifications of snowflakes, each with a specific description and number such as these: *rimed columnar crystal* (R1b), *stellar crystal with needles* (CP3a), or *dendritic crystal with sectorlike ends* (P2d). Despite our best efforts to catalog snowflakes, there is still one classification listed as *miscellaneous* (14). In the book, Libbrecht finally answers the question: "Is it true that there are no two snowflakes alike?" He devotes six pages to his answer, and finally says, "It all depends on what you mean by 'snowflake' and what you mean by 'alike.'"

Reading about snowflakes and looking at pictures of them can increase our appreciation of these wintry beauties. But nothing can compare with going outside in the snow and making snow angels, building a snowperson, sledding or skiing down a snowy hill, waging a snowball fight with your friends, or catching a few flakes on your stuck out, eager little tongue.

For Reflection/Discussion

- ❧ Do you ever take time to play in God's weather?
- ❧ In what ways are you yourself a unique creation of God's?

He gives snow like wool;
he scatters frost like ashes.   ❧ PSALM 147:16

*Designer of Snowflakes, help me to appreciate
a few of life's simple pleasures today.*

36 Flowers

Make room for that which is capable of rejoicing, enlarging, or calming the heart.

> ❧ GERHARDT TERSTEEGEN

When I was growing up on the farm, flowers were as much a part of my life as animals. Near the house we had lilac bushes, snowball bushes, roses, lilies-of-the-valley, daffodils, narcissus, tulips, phlox, white petunias, red salvia, and hydrangea. Hollyhocks sprouted beside the barn while daylilies sprang up in the ditches by the road. In spring, all the trees burst into bloom: flowering crab, pink and white dogwood, apple, cherry, pear, peach, and plum. Indian paintbrushes and daisies dotted the fields out back. And in the woods, there were always patches of May apples and spring beauties, and more rarely, jack-in-the-pulpits and trilliums.

Flowers were more than decorations. They marked time for us. When the lilacs bloomed, we knew school was almost over. When the petunias graced our flower beds and flower boxes, we knew it was summer. And as soon as the hydrangea turned purple, we knew it was almost time to go back to school.

I have often wondered: Why did God make so many different flowers? There is no end to their shapes and colors, not to mention their beauty. We humans pay homage to flowers every time we give them to each other for special occasions or (better yet) for no particular reason at all. And giving cut flowers (as opposed to giving plants) is especially meaningful. Father Demetrius Dumm, my Scripture professor, always maintained that giving cut flowers was the greatest expression of love precisely because it was a gesture of such wild extravagance.

One way we can pay tribute to flowers, then, is by appreciating their beauty. Another way is by appreciating the beauty of their names. And that is how I will end this reflection: simply by listing the names of fifty flowers. Please do not skip the final paragraph. Just read the names slowly and reverently (aloud would be best). If the name conjures up an image or a memory, then sit with that for a minute or two. If it does not, then simply take delight in the colorful name. Here we go:

Rose, daisy, lilac, pansy, peony, creeping phlox, petunia, lavender, forsythia, pussy willow, lily-of-the-valley, foxglove, iris, sagebrush, aster, columbine, myrtle, clematis, geranium, impatiens, hibiscus, violet, shamrock, sunflower, bougainvillea, Queen Anne's lace, Rose of Sharon, Black-eyed Susan, primrose, hosta, spotted nettle, bird of paradise, orchid, indigo, candytuft, variegated sedum, chrysanthemum, amaryllis, trumpet vine, oriental poppy, delphinium, sweet William, snapdragon, zinnia, morning glory, honeysuckle, magnolia, Love-in-a-Mist, ostrich fern, and forget-me-not.

For Reflection/Discussion

- What is your favorite flower and why?
- What role do flowers play in your life?

"And why do you worry about clothing? Consider the lilies of the field, how they grow; they neither toil nor spin, yet I tell you, even Solomon in all his glory was not clothed like one of these." MATTHEW 6:28–29

Extravagant God, thank you for the flowers.

37 Resiliency

Courage is the power to let go of the familiar.

🌶 RAYMOND LINDQUIST

Some things in nature are very resilient. Take cockroaches. (Warning: if you are too squeamish to read about cockroaches, just skip the first three paragraphs of this reflection.) Cockroaches have been around a long time. Some fossils date back 350 million years. One reason these insects have survived so long is because they are omnivores. This means they will eat anything. Some have been known to survive for weeks on the glue of a postage stamp.

Cockroaches are prolific too. In some species, the female needs to be impregnated only once in her lifetime. She can then produce between four hundred and (this is not a typo) a million offspring! Another reason cockroaches are resilient is because they are incredibly adaptable. They can, for example, survive a whole month without food. If they suddenly find themselves trapped underwater, they can hold their breath for forty-five minutes (until another cockroach throws them a line). They have also mastered the art of slowing down their heart beat, a little trick that further contributes to their resiliency. And (this gets a little gross) cockroaches can live up to a month without their heads.

The word on the street is, in the event of a nuclear holocaust, cockroaches will inherit the earth. There is some truth to this. The lethal dose of radiation for cockroaches is six to fifteen times greater than for humans. Fruit flies, however, are virtually radiation-resistant, so they are really the survivors.

Sequoia trees are also very resilient with some of them living to be hundreds or even thousands of years old. These giant trees are seldom toppled by heavy winds because they grow in groves for protection. In addition, the roots of one tree interlock with the roots of the other trees thus anchoring them all securely to the ground and to one another. (Talk about mutual support!) The bark of sequoias is quite thick and thus resistant to harm caused by insects, birds, and other creatures. Sequoia wood barely burns. In fact, it is almost as fireproof as asbestos. A few years back, the top of one sequoia was struck by lightning during a July thunderstorm. The tree stood there quietly smoldering with no apparent harm to it until the fire was put out by an October snowstorm.

Some things in nature, however, are not very resilient. Take pandas. They are on the endangered species list for two main reasons: they eat only bamboo, and female pandas are fertile only a few days of the year. As we know, resiliency has nothing to do with being big either. Case in point: the dinosaurs. Despite their huge size, they did not make it past the Cretaceous Period about sixty-five million years ago. Today we are all worried about the survival of polar bears, and rightfully so. Though one of the largest carnivores on the planet, the polar bear could well become extinct if the arctic ice continues to melt, thus depriving them of their natural habitat.

Where do we humans fall on the resiliency scale? In one way humans are very resilient. Our superior intelligence makes us adaptable. We can adapt to virtually any climate on earth. At this moment, human beings are living on every continent, including Antarctica. We humans have discovered ingenious ways to survive even in space and on the moon. We just pack up our food and our environment and take them along for the trip. Though some humans are picky eaters, most of us can survive on a wide variety of foods: burgers, tofu, rice, beetles, strawberries, lettuce, fish eggs, to name just a few. In the resiliency race, the victory goes to the eclectic eater.

But in another way, we humans are quite low on the resiliency scale. We can survive only a few days without water and not much longer without food. Another factor that diminishes our resiliency is, compared to other species, we have very few offspring. And for the ones we do have, we are forced to invest eighteen or twenty years of our lives to raising. Compare that to many birds who raise several batches of offspring each year and who think nothing of kicking them out of the nest after only a few weeks.

As humans, we are very susceptible to other threats. Over sixty-three million people (roughly three percent of the world population) were killed during World War II alone. (Sometimes the greatest threat to our resiliency is us!) The Bubonic Plague also proved how fragile the human species can be—as did the 1918-19 Influenza Pandemic that killed between twenty and forty million people worldwide in just one year! So, before we pat ourselves on the back for being at the top of the food chain, let us remember: our demise as a species is merely one teeny virus or one small nuclear war away.

For Reflection/Discussion

- How have you experienced your resiliency lately?
- In what ways have you experienced yourself as fragile? What did you learn from this?

Therefore I am content with weaknesses, insults, hardships, persecutions, and calamities for the sake of Christ; for whenever I am weak, then I am strong.

- 2 Corinthians 12:10

Author of Life, make me more aware of my resiliency and fragility and that of the everyone I interact with today.

38 The Spider in My Room

By virtue of the creation and, still more, of the incarnation, nothing here below is profane for those who know how to see.
❧ Pierre Teilhard de Chardin

I had been gone only a week, but as soon as I entered my bedroom, lugging my suitcase behind me, I spotted him: the spider. There he was near the ceiling, sitting on his freshly spun web right out in the open, and he was eyeing me. "The nerve!" I said to myself.

My first impulse was to take my shoe off and send him to spider heaven. But, as all my friends know, I am reluctant to kill just about any living thing. In fact, I have even been known to use business envelopes to scoop up crickets, ants, lady bugs, and other creatures that have wandered into the house and deposit them gently but firmly outside where they belong. So, the appearance of this spider gave me pause.

How could this creature, with a body not much bigger than a sesame seed, bother me so much? For one thing, this was *my* room. Not his. He had no business being in my room. Yet, I reasoned, he was not very big; he did not look very ferocious, and he certainly wasn't poisonous. So I was not actually afraid of him. In fact, I almost found myself pitying the little fellow. What kind of life do spiders have anyway? They spin webs, they eat, they sleep, and they make baby spiders. Not much excitement there. If he had spun his web in some unobtrusive place—like behind the dresser—he could have co-habited with me for months and I would not have minded because I would not have known he was there.

So I made a pact with him. Right then and there. I told him he could stay if he just got out of my sight. "Go behind the dresser or under my bed or into the closet," I told him. "Build your web there. Live your spider life and I'll live my human one and neither of us will bother the other. Agreed?" He must have. Because when I came back to my room later that day, he was gone. Or at least he was out of sight. And I have not seen him since.

For Reflection/Discussion

- ❧ What is your attitude toward insects? Have you ever dialogued with them?
- ❧ How do you usually react to the ordinary nuisances in life?

And God said, "Let the earth bring forth living creatures of every kind: cattle and creeping things and wild animals of the earth of every kind." And it was so. God made the wild animals of the earth of every kind, and the cattle of every kind, and everything that creeps upon the ground of every kind. And God saw that it was good.   ❧ GENESIS 1:24–25

God of All Things, help me to dialogue with the blessings as well as the nuisances in my life.

39 Migration

Savor questions and thrill to the quest.
See your life as a journey that quickens
your faith and deepens your soul.
🕊 FREDERIC AND MARY ANN BRUSSAT

*I*n 1905 my grandmother left her native Bohemia, boarded a ship in Hamburg, and sailed across the Atlantic Ocean to the United States. She was only fifteen years old. Traveling with two girlfriends, Anna left behind her parents, several siblings, and many friends—all of whom she would never see again. My grandmother was one of thirty-five million immigrants who came to the United States between the years 1846 and 1940. Landing in New York City, she entered the country through Ellis Island, a place that processed twelve million immigrants between 1892 and 1954. With about $20 in her pocket, she bought a ticket on a train bound for Cleveland, Ohio, where her older sister, Mary, was waiting for her.

When I reflect on this move by my Grandma Svoboda, I am amazed at her courage and daring. I also see her migration from Bohemia to the United States as one tiny piece in the vast network of migrations the world has seen throughout history and in our own day, migrations not only of humans, but of animals, insects, and birds.

Simply put, migration is the movement of living organisms from one biome to another. Most migrations in the animal world occur because of food shortages or for breeding purposes. Species that migrate regularly include whales, gnus, butterflies, moths, locusts, salmon, eels, and lemmings. Perhaps the most highly publicized animal ever to migrate was a humpback whale dubbed Humphrey that mistakenly entered San Francisco Bay while heading from Mexico to Alaska. Forty feet long and weighing eighty thousand pounds, Humphrey made the same wrong turn into the bay not once but twice—in 1985 and 1990. Both times, amid a flurry of media attention, it took the combined efforts of the Marine Mammal Center, the U.S. Coast Guard, and hundreds of volunteers to save Humphrey by successfully guiding him back out into the Pacific Ocean.

One of the most spectacular migrations in nature is that of birds. Though scientists have studied bird migration for many years, they still cannot fully explain the phenomenon. They suspect both the timing and the general routes of migration are somehow controlled by genetics. But bird migration also seems partly dependent upon certain cognitive skills. Some migrating birds, for example, seem to be able to read the landscape below them like a map. Researchers have also learned it is possible to teach some birds newer and safer migratory routes. Using an ultra-light plane to lead the flocks, they have successfully taught new routes to both Canada geese and whooping cranes.

Birds that rely on thermals for flight (such as birds of prey) cannot migrate over large bodies of water since thermals exist only over land. Some narrow strips of land (like the Straits of Gibraltar) see huge flocks of migratory raptors twice a year simply because these birds are unable to migrate across the Mediterranean Sea. The Bering Straits is another "hot spot" for vast flocks of migrating birds, a sight that avid birders describe simply as breathtaking.

The migratory bird that racks up the most frequent flyer miles is the arctic tern. This bird flies literally from "pole to pole" (from the Arctic to Antarctica) and it does so twice a year! Recently one arctic tern chick was banded on an island off the British coast and in just three months it was found in Melbourne, Australia. That is a flight of over fourteen thousand miles!

A discussion about migration would be incomplete without a word about the monarch butterfly. Monarchs are those beautiful orange and black butterflies that are fairly common in the United States and a few other countries. Before the first frost hits, these butterflies begin their long migration southward to warmer climes. Millions of them winter in the mountainous forest of central Mexico, congregating on trees in clumps as thick as leaves. In spring, they begin their

long journey northward again. Since the journey of the monarch out-lasts their life span (which is only a few months),
the monarchs breed and die along the way. This means that
the monarchs we see in the spring are the descendents of the
ones who departed in the fall. How does a butterfly that has
never made the migratory journey know when to leave and
where to go? This remains a great mystery. The most we can
say is that the secret of migration is somehow encoded in the
monarch's DNA.

In his book, *The Path: A One-Mile Walk through the Universe,* Chet Raymo describes his visit to the Chincua Monarch
Sanctuary in Mexico where he sees for himself the marvel of
"trees festooned with butterflies as thick as jungle foliage."
Upon beholding these twenty million butterflies firsthand,
he is overcome by "a sense of the holy." He writes, "If any
creature embodies within itself the secrets of cosmic complexity, it is the monarch butterfly."

For Reflection/Discussion

- How has migration impacted your life personally?
- What types of migrating creatures have you witnessed—and what was your reaction?

Now the Lord said to Abram, "Go from your country and your kindred and your father's house to the land that I will show you."   Genesis 12:1

God of Every Land, help me to seek
and find you wherever I may journey.

40 Meditation in a Cemetery

Death is not the enemy who puts an end to everything but the friend who takes us by the hand and leads us into the Kingdom of eternal love.

❧ Henri Nouwen

What am I doing in this cemetery? It's Thursday, an ordinary day. Certainly I have better things to do than sit among these tombstones. And yet today, my day off, I felt a gentle urging to come here, to spend a few hours in prayer and to see what this sacred place might teach me about death. And about life. And so, lacing up my sneakers and donning my jacket, I grabbed the few things I sensed I would be needing this afternoon: my journal, a prayer book, and one red apple.

And here I sit on top of a hill with the entire cemetery spread out below me. Already I realize it is a lively place. I see two men shoveling dirt onto several sunken graves. They work slowly, as if they had all the time in the world. But shouldn't cemetery workers know better? No one has all the time in the world. Two other men are cutting the grass near-by. Perched atop their orange lawn mowers, they scurry in and out among the tombstones as if racing against time. They too should know better. None of us ever wins that race. Far-ther away, another man sits atop a yellow tractor equipped with a back hoe. He is digging a fresh grave. Ironically, he and the others make their living off the dead.

There are other ironies. A small cluster of purple violets sprouts beside an old neglected tombstone, their simple beauty adorning the grave of someone long forgotten. Now that I have been sitting here for a while, a few heretofore cau-tious sparrows have grown more daring. They hop within a few feet of me and cock their heads warily, as if trying to decide if I am flesh or granite. I try to make them think I am granite by sitting silent and motionless. But a blink of my eyes betrays my fleshhood and, catching sight of it, the birds fly off.

Then there are the ants. They are far bolder than the birds. Rude actually. Periodically they crawl onto my feet and legs. I brush them off—my brushing a clear sign to them that I am, indeed, still alive. And if they, indeed, want to remain so, they had better stay off me—or else. I know my "or else" is an empty threat though. For, being more flesh than granite,

I would not actually kill them. The ants must sense that, for they keep crawling all over me, and I keep brushing them off—more with annoyance than animosity.

Some of the tombstones are large and ornate with images of Jesus, Mary, or an angel or two. Some have lengthy epitaphs or scripture verses carved into them. Others, by contrast, are very simple. I spot one that is only a small, white wooden cross with the word DAD painted on it in black letters. No name. No date. Just DAD.

But it is the people who come to the cemetery that interest me most: the mourners. Or, as I prefer to call them, the rememberers. First, there is the steady parade of elderly people. Being elderly themselves, they have more time to remember their dead. Perhaps more incentive too.

But soon a young man (maybe twenty-five or so) drives up in a bright blue pickup truck. Wearing jeans and a maroon sweatshirt, he climbs out of his truck, strides unhesitatingly to a certain grave (obviously he has been here before), and stops. Then he squats down—as some men are wont to do when chatting with friends in backyards when no chairs are handy. He stays for a while, squatting the whole time, as if chatting with the person who is buried there—a mother or father maybe? A grandparent, brother, sister, friend? I will never know, but whoever the deceased is, he or she is lucky to be remembered by such a nice young man.

Next a woman, probably in her thirties, arrives in a gray minivan. She gets out and walks down a hill in her dark brown slacks and tan blazer. She stands before a grave with her head bowed and her hands loosely clasped in front of her. By the way she is dressed, I suspect she is on her way somewhere. And yet, conscious of the deeper on-the-wayness of life, she takes a few minutes on this ordinary day to remember someone who has made it all the way.

Other people come. There is a young woman with two small children. She carries the little girl while the little boy skips along beside her. The girl wears a pink jacket and white bonnet. The little boy sports a black and gold Pittsburgh Steeler sweatshirt. At first the children seem out of place among the tombstones. They are so young and innocent, so filled with life. But when I think again, I decide it is never too early to initiate children into the mystery of life, which of course includes death—and our rituals of remembering both.

But of all who come, I like the young woman best. I hear the "varoom" of her car even before I see it cresting the hill. It is a bright red sports car. The car, such a symbol of youthfulness and speed and freedom, seems out of place in the cemetery. But the driver soon proves she is very much at home here.

She parks her car and hops out. She is wearing gray sweats, and her long dark hair, loosely bound in a pony tail, hangs down her back. With her lean figure, she jogs up the hill with ease. She greets the two men who are shoveling dirt onto the sunken graves. They stop their work momentarily and greet her. And for a minute, I think, "She's coming to see *them* not a grave." But she passes on, her goal lying beyond somewhere.

Soon she stops before a large black tombstone and, in clear view of all, she falls on her knees and bows her head in prayer. After a few minutes, she stands up, approaches the tombstone, bends over, and kisses it twice. Then she jogs down the hill, hops into her car, and "varooms" out the cemetery—all in one seamless motion.

Time passes. I jot in my journal. Then, remembering my apple, I take it out of my pocket, polish it on my sleeve, and bite into it. It is sweet, juicy and noisy—just like life. As I chew it, I think about how the flesh of this apple will become my flesh in a deep and real way. And how this apple carries future apples in its seeds. And when I am finished musing and eating, I toss the core into some nearby weeds, saying to myself, "It's okay. The apple is 100% biodegradable—just like me."

Then I open my prayer book searching for more wisdom in God's words. The wisdom is fast in coming. The opening antiphon is: "I cried to you, Lord, and you healed me. I will praise you forever." Whether I am seated on top of the ground like today or buried beneath it tomorrow, I will praise you God—*forever*—for all time and beyond time, right?

And next the psalmist asks: "Can dust give you praise or proclaim your truth?" And I know the answer to that question is a resounding *yes*. For even here in this cemetery, proclamations of God's truth are being made by slow workers and speedy ones, by cautious birds and bold ants, by young men squatting and little boys skipping, by young women in red sports cars, and by red apples filled with juice and seeds.

And the words of Thursday's psalm prayer become my own: "God, our Father, glorious in giving life, and even more glorious in restoring it…, do not turn away from us, or we shall fall back into dust, but rather turn our mourning into joy by *raising us up with Christ.*" With Christ.

I close the book. I finish my prayer, my meditation, my scribbling. It is time to go. Reluctantly I get up and begin to walk back down the hill—more conscious now of how every movement is a step on my journey, through time, through life, through death, and into new life again. With Christ. Yes, with Christ. Amen. Alleluia!

For Reflection/Discussion

- ✖ What is your attitude toward death? Have you ever spent time in a cemetery?
- ✖ How do you communicate with your loved ones who have gone before you into eternal life?

Jesus said to her, "I am the resurrection and the life. Those who believe in me, even though they die, will live, and everyone who lives and believes in me will never die."   ✖ John 11:25–26

God of Life and Death, lead me closer to you
and to my loved ones who are
already with you in eternity.

Index

(The number indicates the number of the reflection.)

Other Books by *Sr. Melannie*

In Steadfast Love
Letters on the Spiritual Life

One of the best spiritual writers of our day offers wonderful collection of letters on the spiritual life. Sr. Melannie believes that no matter what our call in life, we are all dealing with similar challenges: trying to pray, getting along with others, coping with change and loss, reaching out to those in need, balancing work and leisure, and being bearers of hope in a world that desperately needs it.

168 pages | $14.95 | 95-628-9

Traits of a Healthy Spirituality

Sr. Melannie describes twenty indicators of a healthy spirituality, including self-esteem, friendship, courage, tolerance, and forgiveness. Using real-life examples and stories, she invites readers to incorporate these qualities and virtues into their own lives. In addition to her insightful reflections on each topic, she offers questions for reflection and discussion and closing prayers.

144 pages | $12.95 | 22-698-0

With the Dawn Rejoicing
A Christian Perspective on Pain and Suffering

Sr. Melannie herself was recently diagnosed with polymyositis, an uncommon disease in which the auto-immune system begins to attack and destroy healthy cells in the body. It is characterized by painful swelling, muscle weakness, and chronic fatigue. So she knows what she is talking about! This lovely book offers inspiration and encouragement to all who deal daily with chronic pain.

168 pages | $14.95 | 95-699-9